Diversity Activities for Psychology

Valerie Whittlesey
Kennesaw State University

Allyn and Bacon
Boston   London   Toronto   Sydney   Tokyo   Singapore

To Jimmy Mays, Jacquelyn Whittlesey, and Thomas Works for their love and patience.

ISBN 0-205-29638-6

Printed in the United States of America

10 9 8 7 6 5 4 3 2 1   03 02 01 00

Contents

Matrix of Activities and Topics

Activity	Introduction	Physiological	Developmental	Learning	Cognition/Perception	Intelligence	Language	Emotions/Motivation	Personality	Health	Human Sex	Abnormal	Social
1	▓												
2	▓												
3	▓												
4	▓												
5	▓												▓
6	▓				▓			▓					▓
7	▓												
8	▓												
9	▓												
10	▓												
11													
12			▓						▓				▓
13		▓	▓									▓	▓
14			▓										▓
15			▓										▓
16		▓	▓										▓
17	▓		▓										▓
18			▓										▓
19				▓							▓		
20				▓									▓
21				▓									▓
22								▓	▓				
23					▓								
24					▓								
25					▓								
26							▓						▓
27							▓						
28							▓						
29							▓						
30							▓						
31					▓		▓						
32	▓	▓				▓							

Activity	Introduction	Physiological	Developmental	Learning	Cognition/Perception	Intelligence	Language	Emotions/Motivation	Personality	Health	Human Sex	Abnormal	Social
33						▓							
34						▓							
35						▓							
36	▓					▓							
37								▓					
38		▓						▓					▓
39		▓						▓					
40								▓					▓
41		▓						▓					
42		▓						▓					
43									▓				
44									▓				▓
45									▓				
46			▓						▓				▓
47									▓				▓
48									▓				
49									▓				▓
50			▓										
51										▓	▓		
52										▓			
53		▓								▓	▓		
54		▓								▓			
55		▓								▓			
56													
57											▓		
58											▓		
59											▓		▓
60											▓		▓
61										▓	▓		
62											▓		▓
63									▓				▓
64		▓										▓	
65		▓										▓	

Activity	Introduction	Physiological	Developmental	Learning	Cognition/Perception	Intelligence	Language	Emotions/Motivation	Personality	Health	Human Sex	Abnormal	Social
66		■										■	
67												■	■
68												■	
69													■
70													■
71													■
72												■	■
73					■								■
74													■
75													■
76					■								■
77													■
78												■	■

Student Preface

Diversity Activities for Psychology is a student manual designed with you in mind. As our society becomes more diverse, it is important for you to understand this diversity. There are many important reasons for learning about diversity in your psychology class: 1) learning about diversity allows you to be fair and equitable in your interactions with other people, 2) learning about diversity helps prepare you for employment in an increasingly pluralistic society after college, 3) learning about diversity makes psychology more relevant for all students, 4) learning about diversity may encourage students from all backgrounds to enter the psychology profession, 5) learning about diversity will increase your knowledge of psychology, and 6) learning about diversity will enrich your emotional and personal development.

The activities cover topics covered in most psychology textbooks. The activities are cross-referenced by topic. Each activity in the student manual is organized in the following format: 1) the title of the activity, 2) the materials needed for the activity (this item is not included if no materials are needed), 3) instructions to carry out the activity, 4) the concept, theory, or principle addressed by the activity and the goal of the activity, 5) discussion questions for the activity, 6) references and suggested readings. A variety of activities are included: activities for you to complete alone, activities for you to complete with a small group of classmates, and activities for the entire class to complete together. Unless otherwise stated, each activity was written originally by the author.

As you cover the psychology topics in your textbook, your instructor will give you assignments from this manual. There is a separate Instructor's Manual to accompany *Diversity Activities for Psychology* that explains how the activities are to be implemented. This manual will provide you with engaging and thought-provoking activities. These activities will broaden your knowledge by providing you with various cultural, ethnic/racial and gender-related information pertaining to the psychology topics you are covering in class. Although this book focuses on presenting cultural, ethnic/racial, and gender-related activities, some activities also incorporate other important diversity topics (sexual orientation, aging, social class, and learning and physical disabilities). Activities #13, 46, 60, and 72 also address sexual orientation issues. Activities #18, 53, 72, and 78 also address aging issues. Activities #32, 53, 64, 70, and 72 also address social class issues. Activities #13, 72, and 78 also address learning and physical disabilities issues. This manual is designed to help you understand and sensitize you to the differences between us but to also demonstrate the universals among us as human beings!

I would like to thank the following colleagues for their assistance in the development of this book: Grace Galliano, G. W. Hill, IV, Linda Noble, and Michael Reiner, all of Kennesaw State University. Finally, I would like to thank the editorial staff Allyn & Bacon for their patience and assistance.

Activity

1
Neglect of Cultural Variation

Concept and Goal

This activity identifies factors indicating why psychology has neglected to address issues of cultural variation in behavior. This is a small-group activity. In your group, you will counter each of the factors eliminating cultural variation with reasons why providing a cultural perspective is important to psychology. Each group will then present their responses to the statements and prepare the discussion questions for class interaction.

Instructions

For most of its history, psychology has been a science based to a large extent on research conducted by American investigators with middle-class American-Caucasian subjects. Many colleagues have challenged psychologists to take culture more seriously. It is important for us to know what behaviors are universal and what behaviors vary as a function of different cultural experiences. Albert (1988) identifies reasons why we have often neglected to examine cultural variation. As you read her reasons, think of counterreasons of how we can eliminate each concern. As a student of psychology, you should meet the challenge and use the investigation of cultural differences as a means of developing a more accurate science of human behavior for all people.

1) We often take our own assumptions, values, and characteristic ways of perceiving the world for granted until we encounter people from another culture. Our relative lack of such direct experience with persons of other cultures has led to a neglect of how cultures vary.

Counter:

2) Our need to simplify events and to focus only on the simplest causes of a particular behavior may lead us to overlook how society or culture shapes that behavior. This simplification may cause us to ignore cultural variability.

Counter:

3) We sometimes ignore cultural variability because we are afraid to create or reinforce stereotypes or promote discrimination. Closely related is the fact that we may view a focus on cultural differences as incongruent with our society's egalitarian ideas.

Counter:

4) We tend to perceive the recognition of cultural differences as a rejection of the historic American goal of assimilation; our society has subscribed to the melting pot theory.

Counter:

5) The dominant political and economic position of the United States in the world may account for our relative lack of interest in cultural variables. Our power has contributed to independence and often to an isolationist stance. Many American citizens believe that our ways are the best ways. Psychology in the United States may have merely reflected that stance.

Counter:

Discussion Questions

1) Why is it important to recognize cultural diversity?

2) Can you think of a topic that you have covered in psychology in which it may be important to examine other cultural or ethnic groups, because their behavior may differ and/or enrich our understanding of that phenomenon? Explain.

References

Albert, R. D. 1988. The place of culture in modern psychology. In P. Bronstein and K. Quina (eds.), *Teaching a Psychology of People: Resources of Gender and Sociocultural Awareness,* 12–18. Washington, DC: American Psychological Association.

Activity 2

Cultural Values

Concept and Goal

Cross-cultural psychologists have traditionally asserted that many principles of behavior and mental processes described in your introductory psychology text are not necessarily universal. There are cross-cultural (i.e., culture to culture) and multicultural (i.e., the ethnicities within a culture) variations in behavior and mental processes. Also, these psychologists have urged psychology instructors to frame courses in a less ethnocentric fashion, recognizing that the European-American perspective is not necessarily the standard against which all other people are judged and compared. This activity is designed to accomplish that goal. You should answer the items independently, but the class should review and discuss the answers to the statements and the discussion questions.

Instructions

Some statements about behavior in psychology reflect statements of cultural differences. That is, ethnic groups within a society (African-Americans, European-Americans, Hispanic-Americans, Asian-Americans, Native Americans, etc.) or ethnic groups of different societies (Canadians, Brazilians, Italians, French, Egyptians, Kenyans, Japanese, etc.) may vary in their agreement with the statement. Read the following ten statements and indicate which statements reflect statements of cultural values (ethnic groups may vary in their agreement with the statement).

_____ 1) There should be equal justice for rich and poor alike.

_____ 2) Children should be encouraged to sleep alone as soon as possible.

_____ 3) A person should go to a medical doctor to be treated for a physical illness.

_____ 4) Everyone has the right to privacy.

_____ 5) Everyone is entitled to happiness.

_____ 6) A person is innocent until proven guilty.

_____ 7) Children should be weaned from the mother's breast at least by one year of age.

_____ 8) Women should have equal rights to men.

_____ 9) The teenage years are turbulent ones.

_____ 10) Marriage should occur between two people who love each other.

Key

All ten statements reflect statements of cultural values. Although we may agree with many of the statements, people from different ethnic groups may not necessarily agree with the statements.

Discussion Questions

1) Was it easy or difficult to identify the items as cultural value statements? Explain.

2) What does this activity indicate about cultural values?

3) Can you think of other cultural value statements that we as Americans tend to accept as true without question?

References

Berry, J. W., Poortinga, Y, A., Segal, M. H., and Dasen, P. R. 1992. *Cross-cultural psychology: Research and applications*. New York: Cambridge University Press.

Kagitcibasi, C., and Berry, J. W. 1989. Cross-cultural psychology: Current research and trends. *Annual Review of Psychology* 40: 493–531.

Activity

3
Avoiding Sexist and Racist Research

Concept and Goal

Much psychological research incorporates a variety of forms of sexism and racism. This is a small-group activity. You will be exposed to common examples of sexist and racist problems. In your small groups, think of solutions for these common problems when doing experiments in psychology. Then your group will design an experiment while avoiding the common sexist and racist problems that have been identified. Each group should present the solutions to the problems, design an experiment, and prepare the discussion questions for class interaction.

Instructions

As mentioned in your psychology textbook, conducting experiments helps us to determine the causes of a behavior. These experiments should use the scientific approach, which means that the experiments should be objectively conducted. However, when values and attitudes are being evaluated, as is often the case in psychology, it is easy for bias to affect the way an experiment is conducted. Bias can occur at all stages of the experimental process:

1) developing a hypothesis,
2) defining the independent variable (variable manipulated by the experimenter) and dependent variable (behavior resulting from the manipulation of the independent variable),
3) selecting a sample,
4) analyzing and interpreting the data, and
5) drawing conclusions from the data.

This activity is divided into two exercises. In Exercise 1, some common problems that can potentially involve sexist and racist research are presented. Your task is to develop a solution to eliminate that problem in the research process. Although the examples presented at each of the five stages of experimentation are either sexist or racist, examples of both sexism and racism can occur at each of the five stages of experimentation. In Exercise 2, you will design an experiment while avoiding some of the problems you have previously examined.

Exercise 1—Eliminating Common Problems
1) Developing a Hypothesis

Problem: Gender and race stereotypes that are associated with the topic studied can bias the hypothesis that is developed.

Example of sexism: Some studies have defined leadership only in terms of dominance, aggression, and other styles that emphasize characteristics congruent with a male stereotype, so that males are hypothesized to be aggressive or females are hypothesized to not be aggressive.

Solution:

2) Defining the Independent and Dependent Variables

Problem: The independent and dependent variables are given labels that suggest negative evaluations of groups or behaviors that are not traditional.

Example of racism: Ethnic minority groups are sometimes labeled as the "impoverished" or "deficient" group.

Solution:

3) Selecting a Sample

Problem: The gender or race of the participants in an experiment can be related with other personal characteristics of the participants. This can sometimes create a biased sample of participants.

Example of racism: For a study examining the juvenile delinquency behavior of African-Americans (or any other ethnic minority group) compared to white Americans, ethnic minorities may show higher rates of juvenile delinquency. However, this may occur because the socioeconomic status of the African-Americans who formed one sample group is lower than the socioeconomic status of the white Americans who formed the other sample group.

Solution:

4) Data Analysis and Interpretation

a. *Problem:* All gender or race differences found are reported. No report is made when differences are not found; this gives an exaggerated portrayal of the actual data.

Example of sexism: "We tested males and females on the verbal, mathematics, and analytical sections of the Scholastic Aptitude Test, and we found that males and females differed significantly on their math scores."

Solution:

b. *Problem:* Gender or race differences are inaccurately magnified.

Example of sexism: "Although only 24% of women were found to have confidence in their spatial abilities, fully 28% of men had confidence in their spatial abilities."

Solution:

5) Drawing Conclusions

Problem: Results based on one sex or race are generalized to all groups.

Example of racism: Life expectancy rates that are based on white Americans are reported as life expectancy rates for all Americans. There is no mention that life expectancy rates vary by ethnic group.

Solution:

Exercise 2—Experiment Development

You are charged with designing an experiment that addresses an issue related to sex or race. For that experiment, develop a hypothesis, identify and operationalize (define as clearly as possible) your independent and dependent variables, identify and describe the characteristics of your sample(s) clearly, indicate how you expect to analyze and interpret your data, and indicate possible conclusions you will draw based on the results that you hope to find.

Discussion Questions

1) Why do you think there are so many similarities between racism and sexism in conducting biased research?

2) Can you think of ways in which racism and sexism differ? If so, how?

3) Can you think of groups other than women and ethnic minorities that can be discriminated against in psychological research? List them.

References

Denmark, F., Russo, N., Frieze, I., and Sechzer, J. July 1988. Guidelines for avoiding sexism in psychological research. *American Psychologist* 43: 582–585.

Ford, T. E., Grossman, R. W., and Jordan, E. A. 1997. Teaching about unintended racism in introduction to psychology. *Teaching of Psychology* 24: 186–188.

McHugh, M. C., Koeske, R. D., and Frieze, I. H. 1986. Issues to consider in conducting nonsexist psychology: A review with recommendations. *American Psychologist* 41: 879–890.

Activity

4

Sex and Race-Related Journals

Concept and Goal

This is a small-group activity. It will acquaint you with two psychology journals. One journal is devoted to research on the psychology of women and the other journal is devoted to psychological research on an ethnic minority group—African-Americans. Your group should answer questions about an article from each of the journals and then prepare the discussion questions for class interaction.

Materials

Copies of an issue of the *Psychology of Women Quarterly* and the *Journal of Black Psychology*, which are available in most college or university libraries, will be needed. *The Psychology of Women Quarterly* is published by Division 35 of the American Psychological Association and can be ordered from Cambridge University Press, 32 East 57th Street, New York, NY 10022. The *Journal of Black Psychology* is published for the Association of Black Psychologists by Sage Publications, 2455 Teller Rd., Thousand Oaks, CA 91320.

Instructions

A considerable amount of research has indicated that European-American males are perceived as the norm; females and ethnic minorities are considered a deviation from the norm. The best examples of the "male as normative" theme in psychology are the sex and race biases in the psychological research process in hypothesis development, defining variables to study, participant selection, the analysis and interpretation of data, and drawing conclusions from the data. Furthermore, there is a tendency for research conducted by women and/or ethnic minority scholars to be considered less rigorous and valuable than reports by male European-American scholars. There are several journals designed to incorporate research on women and on ethnic minorities into psychology. Two such journals are the *Psychology of Women Quarterly* and the *Journal of Black Psychology*.

First, browse through an issue of the *Psychology of Women Quarterly* and the *Journal of Black Psychology* and answer the following questions for each journal.

1) Who is the general editor of this journal?

2) What is the journal's statement on the content area of the articles published in the journal?

Second, select one research article from each journal and answer the following questions.

1) Which volume and year of the journal did you select?

2) What is the title of the article that you selected?

3) What question, problem, or hypothesis does the author want to investigate?

4) What do you believe is the significance of this topic?

5) Where was the study conducted?

6) What instruments and techniques were used in the study?

7) Who was studied and why?

8) How did the author summarize the findings?

9) Did the findings turn out as the author expected? Why or why not?

10) Does the article contribute to the field of the psychology of women (or to the field of the psychology of African-Americans)?

11) Do you agree with the findings? Explain.

Discussion Questions

1) Why are journals such as the *Psychology of Women Quarterly* and the *Journal of Black Psychology* important to the field of psychology?

2) If you were going to conduct a psychological study on women or ethnic minorities, what topic would you study? Why?

References

Ford, T. E., Grossman, R. W., and Jordan. E. A. 1997. Teaching about unintended racism in introduction to psychology. *Teaching of Psychology* 24: 186–188.

Paludi, M., and Epstein, C. 1990. Feminist and sex-fair methodology. In V. P. Makowsky, C.

C. Sileo, L. G. Whittemore, C. P. Landry, and M. L. Skutley (eds.), *Activities Handbook for the Teaching of Psychology* (Vol. 3). Washington, DC: American Psychological Association.

Wallston, B. S. 1981. What are the questions in the psychology of women? A feminist approach to research. *Psychology of Women Quarterly* 5: 597–617.

Activity 5

Demonstrating Experimentation

Concept and Goal

You will design a field experiment to test and answer a research question related to race and/or gender. This is a class activity. The class will design the experiment and prepare the discussion questions for class interaction.

Instructions

Psychologists seek answers to questions about behavior. The method that psychologists use to answer questions in psychology is experimentation. This is a technique in which we determine causation. We manipulate variables to discover the effects of the manipulation on behavior. Your instructor will ask the class to design a field experiment to test one or both of the following hypothesis: (1) People help white Americans more than black Americans or (2) people help women more than men.

You will need to identify the following components for the experiment:
1) the independent variable (variable manipulated by the experimenter) and the dependent variable (behavior resulting from the manipulation of the independent variable),
2) the operational definitions (clear definitions of the independent and dependent variables),
3) the control variables (the control of variables other than the independent variable that are likely to influence the dependent variable),
4) the procedure for the subjects, and
5) the use of statistical procedures to analyze the data.

The following is an example of a sample experiment to test the hypothesis. After you have read this experiment, the class should design another experiment to test the hypothesis.

Sample Experiment

1) The independent variable is whether the person requesting help is black or white (or whether the person requesting help is male or female). The independent variable is a naturally occurring independent variable in this experiment, since we can't manipulate race (or gender), so there are no experimental and control groups. The dependent variable is helping behavior.

2) An operational definition for helping behavior is whether a subject provides a quarter to a black or white person (or male or female person) who requests it for an emergency call.

3) There are several control variables.
   a) Randomization is necessary; we should randomly select subjects to participate in the experiment to ensure that participants represent a cross-section of ages, races, and genders.

b) The place, day, and time that subjects participate in the experiment should be the same for all subjects.

c) The person who requests the quarter should be black half of the time and white half of the time (or male half of the time and female half of the time). The black and white persons (or the male and female persons) requesting the quarter for an emergency call are assisting the investigator of the experiment, so they are called confederates.

d) All of the confederates should be identical in their behaviors and in the scripts that they give to the subjects; also, there should be the same number of black and white (or male and female) confederates.

4) The following can be a procedure. The confederate can be standing next to a car with a flat tire in which there is no spare tire. The confederate should approach subjects who walk by. Randomization can be achieved by approaching every third person who walks within five feet of the car. The confederate can explain to the subject that the car tire is flat and there is no spare; the confederate can then ask for a quarter to make a call home.

5) A second confederate can be posted nearby in an inconspicuous location to record how many people provide a quarter to the first confederate. The investigator can examine the results. The investigator uses a statistical test to compare the percentage of black (or male) confederates that were helped compared to the percentage of white (or female) confederates.

The class should design another experiment to test the hypothesis that people help white Americans (or females) more than they help black Americans (or men). The experiment should address the five components of experiments mentioned earlier.

Discussion Questions
1) What is the advantage to experimentation in answering questions in psychology?

2) If an experiment were actually conducted and people were found to help one group more than another group, what are the implications?

3) Can you think of any extraneous variables (variables other than the manipulation of the independent variable) in the sample experiment or the experiment designed by the class that may have affected the results?

4) Although identifying the control variables for an experiment is wise to ensure that the independent variable influenced the dependent variable, the use of control variables can create limitations in generalizing the results of an experiment. If the hypothesis is correct, what are possible limitations to the sample experiment and the experiment designed by the class?

5) What would be the expected results if our hypothesis was confirmed? What would be the expected results if our hypothesis was not confirmed?

6) If we wanted to examine whether people help white Americans more than an ethnic group other than black Americans (Chinese-Americans, Hispanic-Americans, Native Americans), how would we alter the experiment?

References

Benjamin, L., and Lowman, K. 1994. Demonstrating experimental design logic. In L. Benjamin and K. Lowman (eds.), *Activities Handbook for the Teaching of Psychology* (Vol. 1). Washington, DC: American Psychological Association.

Eagly, A., and Crowley, M. 1986. Gender and helping behavior: A meta-analytic review of the social psychological literature. *Psychological Bulletin* 100: 283–303.

Gaertner S., and Dovidio, J. 1986. The aversive form of racism. In J. F. Dovidio and S. L. Gaertner (eds.), *Prejudice, Discrimination, and Racism.* Orlando, FL: Academic Press.

Gray, C., Russell, P., and Blockley, S. 1991. The effects upon helping behavior of wearing pro-gay identification. *British Journal of Social Psychology* 30: 171–178.

Watson, D. 1995. A field experiment in helping. In V. P. Makosky, C. C. Sileo, L. G. Whittemore, C. P. Landry, and M. L. Skutley, *Activities Handbook for the Teaching of Psychology* (Vol. 3). Washington, DC: American Psychological Association.

Activity 6

Illusory Correlation

Concept and Goal

This activity demonstrates an illusory correlation, a perceived correlation (relationship between two variables) that does not really exist. This is a class activity. After you have individually answered the questions that the instructor has posed and the instructor has analyzed the data, the class should prepare the discussion questions for class interaction.

Instructions

Your instructor will present 30 pictures to you. Your task is look at each picture as it is presented. After all 30 pictures are presented, the instructor will pose a series of questions to you.

Discussion Questions

1) Did the results of the class's data indicate that females were overly associated with the pictures depicting fright compared to males? If so, explain why it occurred. If there was no gender-related illusory correlation, give possible reasons why it did not occur.

2) Can you think of examples of an actual correlation?

3) Can you think of examples of an illusory correlation?

References

Brody, L. and Hall, J. 1993. Gender and emotion. In M. Lewis and J. Haviland (eds.), *Handbook of Emotions*, 447–460. New York: Guilford.

Chapman, L. J., and Chapman, J. 1967. Genesis of popular but erroneous psychodiagnostic observations. *Journal of Abnormal Psychology* 74:193–204.

Coats, E., and Feldman, R. 1996. Gender differences in nonverbal correlates of social status. *Personality and Social Psychology Bulletin* 22: 1014–1022.

Duclos, S., Laird, J., Sexter, M., Stern, L., and VanLighten, O. 1989. Emotion-specific effects of facial expressions and postures on emotional experience. *Journal of Personality and Social Psychology* 57: 100–108.

Izard, C. 1977. *Human emotions.* New York: Plenum.

Rocklin, T. 1990. A demonstration of the illusory correlation effect. In V. P. Makosky, C. C. Sileo, L. G. Whittemore, C. Landry, and M. L. Skutley (eds.), *Activities Handbook for the Teaching of Psychology* (Vol. 3). Washington, DC: American Psychological Association.

Activity

7   *Early African-Americans and Women*

Concept and Goal

This activity is an individual student activity; it is designed to familiarize you with some of the earlier African-Americans and women in psychology and their contributions to the field of psychology. After you have researched the psychologist you are assigned, each student will perform a role-play of their psychologist to the class. Then prepare the questions for class interaction.

Instructions

Select one of the African-American or women psychologists from the list below and prepare a role play presentation for class. Include the following information about the psychologist you select.

1) Name
2) Date of birth
3) Specific contributions(s) to the field and date(s) if known
4) Significant events occurring during the lifetime or at the time of major contribution
5) Overall contributions to the field

Role Play Samples

Martin David Jenkins (1904–1978)

I am MARTIN DAVID JENKINS. I was born in 1904 in Terre Haute, Indiana. I received the Ph.D. degree in educational psychology from Northwestern University in 1935. My dissertation, A Socio-Psychological Study of Negro Children of Superior Children, "showed that the proportion of gifted black children was about the same as that for gifted white children, provided that equal educational opportunities were provided" (p. 80). I identified a representative sample of superior black students, one of whom has an IQ of 200, the highest on record at that time. During my professional life, I served a professor, dean, and college president. While psychologists were questioning the equality of intelligence test scores of African-Americans and white Americans, I conducted research that was especially significant because it "provided authenticated data that counteracted popular beliefs of Black inferiority and underlined the importance of testing rapport" (p. 80).

Guthrie, R.V. (1998). *Even the rat was white: A historical view of psychology* (2nd ed.). Boston: Allyn & Bacon.

Nancy Bayley (1899-)

I am NANCY BAYLEY. I was born in 1899. I am a developmental psychologist, most noted for the development of the Bayley Scales of Infant Development. This test has been described by Anne Anastasi as "an especially well-constructed test for the earliest age levels" (p. 237). The first edition, published in 1969, was an outgrowth of the Berkeley Growth

Study in which I participated. The test is now in this second edition, the Bayley-II, published in 1993. My associates and I established norms for the Bayley-II on 1700 children —50 males and 50 females in each of 17 age groups between 1–42 months. We made sure that the standardization sample represented the U.S. population according to race/ethnicity, major geographical area, and parental educational level. As a result of my work, I was the first woman to receive the American Psychological Association Distinguished Scientific Contribution Award in 1966. I believe my test made a major contribution to the field of testing as one of the forerunners of infant testing. It has been helpful in the early detection of sensory and neurological defects, emotional disturbances, and environmental defects. I must admonish you, however, to be sure to use it primarily to assess current developmental status, since it is not a good predictor of later abilities.

Anastasi, A., and Urbina, S. 1997. *Psychological testing.* 7th ed. Upper Saddle River, NJ: Prentice-Hall.

Cohen, R. J., Montague, P., Nathanson, L.S., and Swerdlik, M. E. 1988. *Psychological testing: An introduction to tests and measurement.* Mountain View, CA: Mayfield.

Some Outstanding African-American Contributors to Psychology

J. Henry Alston	Martin David Jenkins
James Arthur Bayton	Reginald L. Jones
Albert Sidney Beckham	Howard Hale Long
John Henry Brodhead	John McAdoo
Herman George Canady	James Thomas Morton, Jr.
Kenneth Bancroft Clark	Carolyn Payton
Mamie Phipps Clark	Inez Beverly Prosser
Paul I. Clifford	Roderick Wellington Pugh
Juanita Collier	Shearley Oliver Roberts
William Cross, Jr.	Margaret B. Spencer
Robert Prentiss Daniel	Francis Cecil Sumner
Alonzo Davis	Charles Henry Thomas
Oral Wendle Eagleson	Charles W. Thompson
Carlton Benjamin Goodlett	Alberta Banner Turner
Edmund Gordon	Frederick Payne Watts
Robert V. Guthrie	Robert L. Williams
Asa Hilliard	Roger Kenton Williams
Ruth Winifred Howard (Beckham)	Howard Emery Wright

Some Outstanding Women Contributors to Psychology

Mary Ainsworth	Edna Heidbreder
Louise Bates Ames	Leta Stetter Hollingworth
Anne Anastasi	Karen Horney
Magda Arnold	Ruth Horowitz
Grace Arthur	Mary Cover Jones

Helen Astin
Harriet Babcock
Katherine Banham
Nancy Bayley
Lauretta Bender
Jean Block
Olga Louise Bridgman
Augusta Bronner
Charlotte Buhler
Mary Whiton Calkins
Psyche Cattell
Ethel Cornell
Florence Denmark
June Downey
Elizabeth Duffy
Ava Champney English
Sybille Escalona
Grace Fernald
Else Frenkel-Brunswik
Anna Freud
Frieda Fromm-Reichmann
Eleanor Gibson
Carol Gilligan
Florence Goodenough
Margaret Harlow
Molly Harrower

Grace Kent
Christine Ladd-Franklin
Blanche Learned
Edith Lord
Eleanor Maccoby
Dorothea McCarthy
Maud Amanda Merrill
Catherine Cox Miles
Christiana Morgan
William Mae (Mollie) Cook Mowrer
Lois Barclay Murphy
Roselie Raynor
E. Louisa Rhine
Anne Roe
Amanda Rohde
Virginia Staudt Sexton
Carolyn Wood Sherif
Janet Taylor Spence
Emmy Sylvester
Clara Thompson
Thelma Thurstone
Leona Tyler
Margaret Floy Washburn
Helen Thompson Wooley
W. C. Wyrwicka

Discussion Questions

1) What did you learn about the psychologist(s) that you role-played in class?

2) What did you learn about the other psychologists that were role played by other students in class?

3) Do you think the contributions of African-American and women psychologists shape the field? If so, explain how.

References

Butler, B. L. February 1998. *Incorporating African-Americans and women into the introduction to psychology course*. Paper presented at the Tenth Southeastern Conference on the Teaching of Psychology, Kennesaw State University.

Corsini, R. J. (ed.). 1990. *Encyclopedia of psychology*. New York: John Wiley.

Fancher, R. 1990. *Pioneers of psychology*. 2nd ed. New York: Norton.

Guthrie, R. V. 1998. *Even the rat was white: A historical view of psychology*. 2nd ed. Boston: Allyn & Bacon.

Kimble, G. A., Wertheimer, M., and White, C. L. 1991. *Portraits of pioneers in psychology*. Washington, DC: APA; Hillsdale, NJ: Lawrence Erlbaum Associates.

O'Connell, A. N., and Russo, N. F. 1983–1988. *Models of achievement: Reflections of eminent women in psychology* (Vols. 1–2). New York: Columbia University Press.

Street, W. R. 1994. *A chronology of noteworthy events in American psychology*. Washington, DC: APA.

Viney, W., and King, D. B. 1998. *A history of psychology: Ideas and context*. 2nd ed. Boston: Allyn & Bacon.

Zusne, L. 1984. *Biographical dictionary of psychology*. Westport, CT: Greenwood.

Other biographical references are American men of science, American men and women of science, American Psychological Association Dictionary, Notable black women, and Who's Who among African-Americans.

Activity

8   *Prominent Women*

Concept and Goal

You will read facts about some of the contributions of women to the field of psychology; the contributions of some of these prominent women in psychology have not been visibly recognized. You should answer the matching items and find additional contributions of women from your textbook. Then the class should review and discuss the matching items, and discuss the additional women contributors found in the textbook and the discussion questions.

Instructions

Match each of the following statements with the appropriate woman psychologist using your psychology textbook as a reference; place the appropriate letter in the space provided. Answers to the matching exercise are provided. After you have completed the matching activity, list women psychologists not mentioned in the activity that are presented in your textbook and indicate their contributions.

_____ 1) She developed the stranger situation—a laboratory technique used in developmental

psychology designed to study the attachment between a mother and baby.

_____ 2) She and her husband did research with rhesus monkeys which indicated that contact

comfort is important in attachment.

_____ 3) She disagreed with Freud's theory of inherent personality differences between women and

men and instead proposed that all neurosis is culture dependent.

_____ 4) She developed the visual cliff test—a device used in developmental psychology to

determine if infants can perceive depth.

_____ 5) She did important gerontological research and identified five predicable stages that people

experience when facing death.

_____ 6) She did pioneering sex research with her husband, William Masters, during the 1960s.

Women Psychologists

a. Elizabeth Kubler-Ross   c. Margaret Harlow   e. Mary Ainsworth
b. Elizabeth Gibson   d. Karen Horney   f. Virginia Johnson

Other Prominent Women (mentioned in your general psychology text)

Name   Contribution

1. _____   _____

2. _____   _____

3. _____   _____

4. _____   _____

5. _____   _____

Key to the Matching Activity
     1.   E.
     2.   C.
     3.   D.
     4.   B.
     5.   A.
     6.   F.

Discussion Questions
1)   What facts did you learn from this activity?

2)   Is this kind of activity important (beneficial)? Why or why not?

3) There is a division of the American Psychological Association (the major professional organization in psychology) known as the Psychology of Women. What purpose do you think this division serves for the field of psychology?

References

Kalat, J. 1999. *Introduction to psychology.* 5th ed. Pacific Grove, CA: Brooks Cole.
Myers, D. 1998. *Psychology* 5th ed. New York: Worth.
Wood, S., and Wood, E. 1999. *The world of psychology.* 3rd ed. Boston, MA: Allyn & Bacon.

Activity
9
Web Hunting for Diversity

Concept and Goal

This activity provides an introduction to the Internet and the World Wide Web and it familiarizes you with some Web sites that incorporate diversity into field of psychology. You will be paired with a classmate to explore the Web and complete the scavenger hunt. Each student pair should discuss their experiences on the Web and prepare the discussion questions for class interaction.

Introduction

The Internet is a global network connecting millions of computers throughout the world. There is a lot of useful information available on the Internet in a wide variety of disciplines including psychology, sociology, anthropology, education, communications, and other areas. The Web can be a particularly useful and powerful culture-learning tool. Some psychology-related culture-learning Web sites are listed below. Your assignment is to partner with one other person and connect to these sites. You can connect to the Web pages by typing an address into your Web browser. After you have visited all five Web sites, select one of the scavenger hunts and complete it.

1)   http://www.worldculture.com/
This site contains lots of interesting information including world capitals, consulates, embassies, cuisine, currency exchange rates, job opportunities, holidays, and many other resources.

Scavenger hunt: Find the languages spoken for all the countries in South America.

2)   http://www.fit.edu/CampusLife/clubs-org/iaccp/
This is the homepage for the International Association for Cross-Cultural Psychology. It contains lots of good information and links.

Scavenger hunt: Find the latest issue of the *Cross-Cultural Psychology Bulletin*. Write down the title and author of an article from that issue.

3)   http://www.cpa.ca/
This is the homepage for the Canadian Psychological Association. It contains good cross-cultural links.

Scavenger hunt: Write down the name of an article from last summer's issue of *Psynopsis*, the Canadian Psychological Association's newspaper.

4) http://www.abpsi.org
This is the homepage for the Association of Black Psychologists, the professional organization for African-American psychologists.

Scavenger hunt: Write down the date and place of the next (or last) Association of Black Psychologists National Convention.

5) http://www.apa.org
This is the homepage for the American Psychological Association. If you select the public area option, you can then access the public interest programs. It contains psychological knowledge and information on programs that address issues of culture, social class, race/ethnicity, gender, sexual orientation, age, and discrimination.

Scavenger hunt: Find the name and price of a book published by the American Psychological Association that relates to one or several ethnic minority groups (Hispanic-Americans, Asian-Americans, Native Americans, African-Americans, etc.).

Discussion Questions

1) What did you learn by visiting the sites listed in this activity?

2) What other information beyond this assignment would you like to search for on the Web related to diversity in psychology?

References

Gardiner, H. 1998. Adventures in cyberspace. In T. M. Singelis (ed.), *Teaching about Culture, Ethnicity, and Diversity: Exercises and Planned Activities.* Thousand Oaks, CA: Sage.

Gilster, P. 1996. *Finding it on the Internet: The Internet navigator's guide to research tools and techniques.* 2nd ed. New York: John Wiley.

Hill, G. W., and Grimes, T. August 1997. *Some resources for teaching cross-cultural and ethnic issues in psychology.* Paper presented at the American Psychological Association meeting, Chicago, IL.

Activity

10

Diversity Jeopardy

Concept and Goal

This activity is a class activity that allows you to learn concepts and information about various ethnic American cultures by either developing a simulated Jeopardy television show session or by serving as a contestant. Approximately five students will develop the Diversity Jeopardy game; the remainder of the class will serve as individual contestants. After the game, the class should prepare the discussion questions for class interaction.

Instructions

Your instructor will assign you to either assist in developing a procedure and questions for the individual contestants (members of the class) or to be a contestant for the game Diversity Jeopardy. Diversity Jeopardy is based on the Jeopardy television show.

Developers: Your instructor will provide you with some answers and questions for the diversity category, Latin-American Psychology. Make up answers and questions for three additional diversity categories, African-American Psychology, Asian-American Psychology and Native American Psychology; the questions can be arranged in terms of difficulty and placed on cards or overhead transparencies. Arrange for contestants (the remainder of the class) to play by developing contestant instructions and a scoring system. You may use the books listed in the reference section to develop the Diversity Jeopardy questions, but you are not limited to those references.

Contestants: Prior to serving as a contestant, review chapters from the books listed in the references or from similar books; this will provide you with background information to assist you as a contestant. Your classmates who are developing the Diversity Jeopardy game will give you contestant instructions. Good luck!

Discussion Questions

1) What facts did you learn about Latin-American psychology?

2) What facts did you learn about African-American psychology?

3)   What facts did you learn about Asian-American psychology?

4)   What facts did you learn about Native American psychology?

5)   Did this activity trigger a desire to acquire other information not covered during this game? If so, what additional information would you like?

References

Jenkins, A. H. 1995. *Psychology and African-Americans: A humanistic approach.* 2nd ed. Boston: Allyn & Bacon.

Monteiro, K. 1995. *Ethnicity and psychology.* Dubuque, IA: Kendall/Hunt Publishing Company.

Ramirez, M. 1983. *Psychology of the Americas.* Elmsford, NJ: Pergamon Press.

Activity

11   *Infant Sleep Arrangements*

Concept and Goal

This activity examines the infant sleeping arrangements of various cultures and how these sleeping arrangements are a result of cultural views of appropriate child development. You should read the passage and then prepare the discussion questions for class interaction.

Instructions

Read the following passage from Laura Berk's *Child Development,* 4th edition (1997) and then answer the discussion questions.

Cultural Variations in Infant Sleeping Arrangements

While awaiting the birth of a new baby, American middle-class parents typically furnish a special room as the infant's sleeping quarters. Initially young babies may be placed in a bassinet or cradle in the parents' bedroom for reasons of convenience, but most are moved by three to six months of age. Many adults in the United States regard this nighttime separation of baby from parent as perfectly natural. Throughout this century, childrearing advice from experts has strongly encouraged it. For example, Benjamin Spock, in each edition of *Baby and Child Care* from 1945 to the present, states with authority, "I think it is a sensible rule not to take a child into the parents' bed for any reason" (Spock & Rothenberg, 1992, 213).

Yet parent-infant "cosleeping" is common around the globe, even in industrialized societies, as a recent comparison of five culturally diverse groups of 6- to 48-month-olds revealed.

Percentage of Cosleeping of
6- to 48-Month-Old Children among Five Cultures

Japanese	59%
African-American	59%
Italian	41%
Caucasian-American—urban	19%
Caucasian-American—breastfed	16%

Japanese children usually lie next to their mothers through infancy and early childhood and continue to sleep with a parent or other family member until adolescence (Takahashi, 1990). Cosleeping is also frequent in some American subcultures. African-American children are more likely than Caucasian-American children to fall asleep with parents and to remain with them for part or all of the night (Lozoff et al., 1995). Appalachian children of eastern Kentucky typically sleep with their parents for the first two years (Abbott, 1992). Among the Mayan of rural Guatemala, mother-infant cosleeping is interrupted only by the birth of a new baby, at which time the older child is moved beside the father or to another bed in the same room (Morelli et al., 1992).

Available household space plays a minor role in infant sleeping arrangements. Dominant child-rearing beliefs are much more important. In one study, researchers interviewed middle-class American and Guatemalan Mayan mothers about their sleeping practices. American mothers frequently mentioned the importance of early independence training, preventing bad habits, and ensuring their own privacy. In contrast, Mayan mothers explained cosleeping helps build a close parent-child bond, which is necessary for children to learn the ways of people around them. When told that American infants sleep by themselves, Mayan mothers reacted with shock and disbelief, stating that it would be painful for them to leave their babies alone at night (Morelli et al., 1992).

Infant sleeping practices affect other aspects of family life. Sleep problems are not an issue for Mayan parents. Babies doze off in the midst of ongoing social activities, are carried to bed, and nurse on demand without waking the mother. In the United States, getting young children ready for bed often requires an elaborate ritual that consumes a good part of the evening. Many American infants and preschoolers insist on taking security objects to bed with them—a blanket or teddy bear that recaptures the soft, tactile comfort of physical closeness to the mother. In societies in which caregivers are continuously available to babies, children seldom develop these object attachments (Wolf & Lozoff, 1989). Perhaps bedtime struggles, so common in American middle-class homes but rare elsewhere in the world, are related to the stress young children feel when they are required to fall asleep without assistance (Kawasaki et al., 1994).

Discussion Questions

1) According to the passage, what is the largest factor contributing to the cultural differences in sleeping arrangements? Can you think of factors not mentioned in the passage that may contribute to differences in infant sleeping arrangements? If so, list them.

2) If infant sleeping practices are part of larger cultural beliefs in a society, how would you describe Japanese, Mayan, and Appalachian views of babies and how appropriate development of the child occurs? How do their views differ from the traditional American view of appropriate child development?

3) Has this article affected your view of whether babies should sleep alone? Explain.

References

Abbott, S. 1992. Holding on—pushing away: Comparative perspectives on the Eastern Kentucky child-rearing practice. *Ethos* 20: 33–65.

Berk, L. 1997. *Child development*. 4th ed. Needham Heights, MA: Allyn & Bacon.

Kawasaki, S., Nugent, J. K, Miyashita, H., Miyashita, H., and Brazelton, T. B. 1994. The cultural organization of infants' sleep. *Children's Environments* 11: 135–141.

Lozoff, B., Wolf, A., Latz, S., and Paludetto, R. March 1995. *Cosleeping in Japan, Italy, and the U.S.: Autonomy versus interpersonal relatedness*. Paper presented at the biennial meeting of the Society for Research in Child Development, Indianapolis.

Morelli, G., Rogoff, B., Oppenheim, D., and Goldsmith, D. 1992. Cultural variation in infants' sleeping arrangements: Questions of indepenence. *Developmental Psychology* 31: 180–197.

Spock, B., and Rothenberg, M. B. 1992. *Dr. Spock's baby and child care*. New York: Pocket

Books.

Takahashi, K. 1990. Are the key assumptions of the "Strange Situation" procedure universal? A view from Japanese research. *Human Development* 33: 23–30.

Wolf, A., and Lozoff, B. 1989. Object attachment, thumbsucking, and the passage to sleep. *Journal of the American Academy of Child and Adolescent Psychiatry* 28: 287–292.

Activity

12

Perceptions of Infants

Concept and Goal

This activity demonstrates whether gender affects parents' perceptions of infants and their traits. This is a class activity. Students will individually have parents rate the traits in the handout. The class will discuss the results and the discussion questions.

Instructions

Rubin, Provenzano, and Luria (1974) report that parents attribute traits to their newborns based on the newborn's sex. This activity asks parents to rate their newborns on a set of traits. Give these traits to a group of parents who have newborn children (birth to 1 year of age) and ask them to rate their newborns (Handout 1). Try to get an equal number of parents who have male vs. female newborns.

Your instructor will give you instructions to complete the activity.

Discussion Questions

1) Did the results from your data indicate that parents vary in their trait attributions of their male and female infants? If so, explain the nature of the differences and why they exist. If gender did not affect trait perceptions, give possible reasons why it did not.

2) In the subfield of social psychology, there is a theory known as the self-fulfilling prophecy. The self-fulfilling prophecy states that our own attitudes and behaviors can affect the actions of others; we by our attitudes and behaviors may produce the actions that we incorrectly interpret as indicating another person's deep-seated personality traits. How does the self-fulfilling prophecy theory have implications if parents perceive gender differences in the traits that their infants have?

References

Rubin, J. Z., Provenzano, F. J., and Luria, Z. 1974. The eye of the beholder: Parents' view on sex of newborns. *American Journal of Orthopsychiatry* 44: 512–519.

Stern, M., and Karraker, K. 1989. Sex stereotyping of infants: A review of gender labeling studies. *Sex Roles* 20: 501–522.

Handout 1
Rating Newborns

1.	1 Firm	2	3	4	5 Soft
2.	1 Big	2	3	4	5 Little
3.	1 Weak	2	3	4	5 Strong
4.	1 Delicate	2	3	4	5 Hardy
5.	1 Well- Coordinated	2	3	4	5 Awkward
6.	1 Assertive	2	3	4	5 Timid
7.	1 Beautiful	2	3	4	5 Plain
8.	1 Calm	2	3	4	5 Excited

Data Worksheet: Rating Newborns

Infant Sex: _____ M _____ F

Infant Age: _____ months

#1- Firm–Soft trait score _____
#2- Big–Little trait score _____
#3- Weak–Strong trait score _____
#4- Delicate–Hardy trait score _____
#5- Well-coordinated–Awkward trait score _____
#6- Assertive–Timid trait score _____
#7- Beautiful–Plain trait score _____
#8- Calm–Excited trait score _____

For each parent, add #1, 2, 5, and 6, and compute a mean score (A); then add #3, 4, 7, and 8, and compute a mean score (B)

Male infants' mean score A _____   Male infants' mean score B _____
Female infants' mean score A _____   Female infants' mean score B _____

Activity

13   *Life's Circumstances*

Concept and Goal

This activity helps you relate the literature on developmental psychology to the everyday experiences of children or parents. In the scenarios, you may need to take the perspective of a person of another ethnic group, of the opposite sex, and/or with a disability. In this activity, you also learn about local agencies that can help you with particular life circumstances. This is a small-group activity. Each group should present the findings of the report to the class. The class should then discuss the discussion questions.

Instructions

You will be assigned to a group of about five students by your instructor and given a scenario about an individual who is dealing with a particular life circumstance. You may focus on the challenges facing the parents, the child, or both. You should choose one of the following aspects of development to address: personality development, academic achievement, physical development, cognitive development, sexual identity, or social relationships. Your group should research the life circumstance and then prepare an oral and/or written report. In addition to doing library research for your report, you can also do an investigation of community resources that may be relevant to your life circumstance.

Discussion Questions

1)   What did you learn about the particular circumstance you researched?

2)   As a parent, what would you do in the particular circumstance? As a child, what would you do in the particular circumstance?

3)   If you had to take the perspective of a person of another ethnic group, another sex, and/or with a disability, what did you learn from that experience?

References

Hamill, S. B., and Hale, C. 1996. Your lot in life. *Teaching of Psychology* 23: 245–246.

Activity

14 *Adult-Child Essay Exchange*

Concept and Goal

This activity helps you understand the social and sex-role development of male and female grade school students. This is an individual student activity. After you have prepared your essay responding to the questions outlined in the activity, you are to present a brief summary of your essay to the class. The class can then review the discussion questions.

Instructions

Your instructor will interview two groups of children: female grade school students and male grade school students. Think of questions that your instructor should ask the children, so that your class can gain an understanding of the interests, concerns, behaviors, motivations, and desires of these students, then predict the two groups' likely responses for later comparison. Base your predictions on the literature you read in the textbook from the section on social development during childhood; include in your readings the topic of gender socialization. The instructor will also have the two groups of children ask questions of you. After the instructor has interviewed the two groups and has provided answers to the children's questions, write an essay responding to the following questions.

1) How did each group's answers help you understand them better?
2) How did what you learned from their answers supplement or make clearer what you have learned in this course? Were you surprised by some of each group's answers? Which specific responses surprised you and why? What had you predicted? How were the females and males similar and different in their responses?
3) How would you answer the questions the children posed to you?

Discussion Questions

1) What did you learn about the interests, concerns, behaviors, motivations, and desires of the children in general?

2) What did you learn about the interests, concerns, behaviors, motivations, and desires of the males in particular? Of the females?

3)   What did you learn from the questions that the two groups asked of you?

References

Kalat, J. 1999. *Introduction to psychology.* 5th ed. Pacific Grove, CA: Brooks Cole.

Katz, L. 1996. Essay exchange with children. An exercise for the child development class. *Teaching of Psychology* 23: 112–115.

Matlin, M. 1999. *Psychology.* 3rd ed. Fort Worth, TX: Harcourt Brace.

Myers, D. 1998. *Psychology.* 5th ed. New York: Worth.

Weiten, W. 1998. *Psychology themes and variations.* 4th ed. Pacific Grove, CA: Brooks Cole.

Wood, S., and Wood, E. 1999. *The world of psychology.* 3rd ed. Boston, MA: Allyn & Bacon.

Activity

15 — *Television Portrayals*

Concept and Goal

This activity demonstrates the gender stereotyping prevalent in preschool children's television viewing behavior. Specifically, the activity examines which television programming presents the most aggressive behaviors, how the male and female characters are portrayed, and the kinds of television shows that preschool boys and girls watch. This is a class activity.

Instructions

Your instructor will assign you to one of two groups: (1) to complete aggression and prosocial behavior counts of commercial and PBS children's programs, or (2) to interview male and female preschoolers about the most popular children's shows and characters. For group one, Worksheet 1 is provided to record your observations of half an hour of either (a) a PBS children's show (e.g., Barney, Sesame Show, Mr. Rogers) or (b) a commercial children's show (e.g., Bugs Bunny, Ninja Turtles, Road Runner). For group two, equal numbers of male and female preschool children (age 2–6) should be interviewed using Worksheet 2. Record whether the child is male or female, which television shows the child watches, and which characters he or she likes best. Also, ask each child why he or she likes the shows and characters listed. Then analyze the results and review the discussion questions.

Discussion Questions

1) Are there any differences between PBS and commercial television children's shows in their aggressiveness? What is the ratio of male and female characters in the shows? Are there differences between the male and female characters in their level of aggressiveness?

2) In general, what kinds of television shows do the preschoolers watch? Are there any differences in television viewing by male and female preschool children? Are there any differences in their preferences for aggressive characters and shows? If so, explain the nature of the difference.

3) Given these findings, what would be your recommendations to parents regarding their preschool children and children's television programs?

References

Friedrich, L. K., and Stein, A.H. 1973. Aggressive and prosocial TV programs and the natural behavior of preschool children. *Monographs of the Society for Research in Child Development* 38 (Vol. 4, Serial No. 151).

Huston, A., Wright, J., Rice, M., Kerkman, D., and St. Peters, M. 1990. Development of television viewing patterns in early childhood: A longitudinal investigation. *Developmental Psychology* 26: 409–420.

Sternglanz, S. H. and Serbin, L. A. 1974. Sex-role stereotyping in children's television programming. *Developmental Psychology* 10: 710–715.

Worksheet 1: Observations of Preschool Children's Television

1. Name of TV Show:

2. TV Network:

3. Brief Summary of the Show:

    _____

    _____

    _____

4. Number of physically aggressive acts: _____

5. Number of verbally aggressive acts: _____

6. Number of physically prosocial acts: _____

7. Number of verbally prosocial acts: _____

8. A. Number of male characters: _____

    B. Characterization of leading male characters:

    Character 1 (circle one)   strong   weak

    Character 2 (circle one)   strong   weak

9. A. Number of female characters: _____

    B. Characterization of leading female characters:

    Character 1 (circle one)   strong   weak

    Character 2 (circle one)   strong   weak

10. Number of sex unidentified (e.g., animal with neutral name) major characters: _____

Worksheet 2: Preschool Children's Television and Character Preferences

Sex of Child _____ Male _____ Female

1. What are your favorite television shows?

_____

_____

_____

_____

2. What characters do you like best?

_____

_____

_____

_____

3. Why do you like these shows and characters?

_____

_____

_____

_____

Activity

16 *Puberty Rites of Passage*

Concept and Goal

This activity encourages you to examine elements common to many rites of passage in nonwestern cultures. Also, it allows you to examine how Western and nonwestern cultures vary in the extent of presence of clearly defined rituals. Read the passages. Then, in small groups, identify elements common to many of the rites of passage for the cultures presented and prepare the discussion questions for class interaction.

Instructions

In many cultures, particularly nonwestern cultures, the transition from childhood to adulthood is marked by some sort of public recognition, or rites of passage. Rites of passage are ceremonies or rituals that recognize or symbolize an individual's movement from one status to another. These coming-of-age experiences vary significantly from one culture to another but are found in most nonindustrialized societies. Puberty rites publicize the attainment of adult status and enhance the mate value of the initiate. Puberty rites of passage in western cultures are not marked by such clearly defined rituals. In fact, some psychologists say that there are no true rites of passage experienced by all members of western society that mark becoming an adult. Rather there are a variety of informal events that mark the transition into adulthood in western cultures such as ours. The following are descriptions of specific rites of passage as they are performed in seven nonwestern cultures. After you have read these descriptions, identify three or four elements that seem common to many of the rites of passage.

The Okiek

The Okiek are a tribal people of Kenya. Their rite of passage ceremony is similar for girls and for boys, ages 14 to 16, though the genders are initiated separately. The initiates are first ceremonially circumsized. After circumcision, youths live in seclusion from adults of the opposite sex for 4 to 24 weeks. They paint themselves with white clay and charcoal in order to appear as wild creatures (cemaasiisyek). Certain secret knowledge is imparted by same-sex elders. The most important knowledge concerns the cemaasiit—a mythical beast that haunts the initiates during their time in seclusion. At night its roar can be heard. The initiation is complete when each youth has seen and held the instrument used for producing the roar and then the youth uses the instrument to produce the roar.

Iria

The Iria is a rite performed by the females of the African Okrika tribe. Girls from the ages of 14 to 16 enter into fatting rooms where they are fed rich local foods to make the body come out. They are taught by the elderly women of the egbelereme society to sing the traditional Iria songs. It is believed among the Iria people that young girls form romantic attachments to water spirits. Before they are considered marriageable and allowed to receive mortal suitors, they must first free themselves from these attachments. This is accomplished by the coming together of the girls at the river on successive dawns to sing the songs they have learned. On the final day, the initiates return to the riverbank and the water spirits are expected to attempt to seize the girls by force. This can be prevented by the Osokolo, a member of owuper society (the male counterpart of the egbelereme). He strikes the girls with sticks, driving them back to the village, ensuring both their safety and future fertility.

Ferta das Mocas Novas

Ferta das Mocas Novas is an initiation into womanhood traditionally performed by the Tukuna people of the Northwest Amazon. It begins with the onset of menstruation, and over the next 4 to 12 weeks, the initiate remains in seclusion in a small chamber constructed within the dwelling of the family for this purpose. During this period, the initiate is thought to be in the underworld and in ever-increasing danger from the Noo, which are demons. For the climax of the rite, guests arrive and some don masks, allowing them to become incarnations of the Noo. For two more days, the initiate remains in the seclusion chamber, her body painted with black genipe dye as protection from the Noo. On the morning of the third day, she emerges from the chamber. Surrounded and protected by relatives, she is led out into the festivities. The family dances with her until dawn, at which time the dancing stops. The initiate is then given a fire brand by a shaman and instructed to throw it at the Noo. This done, the power of the Noo is broken, and the Tukuna female is safely entered into womanhood.

Vision Quest

The vision quest is common to many tribes that are native of North America. It is performed as a rite of passage for adolescent males, but not exclusively so. It begins with the bringing of a boy, 14 or 15 years of age, into the sweat lodge. There, his body and spirit are purified by the heat from the burning of cedar. With him in the sweat lodge, is a medicine man to advise and assist him with his prayers. Afterwards, he is taken to an isolated spot and left there to fast for four days. There he will pray, contemplate the words of the medicine man, and await a vision which will reveal to him his path in life as a man in native society.

Kaguru

The Kaguru is a tribe in eastern Africa. Ten and twelve-year-old boys in the Kaguru tribe are led into the bush, stripped of all clothing, and ritually circumcised while being taught the sexual practices of adulthood of male members of the community. Later, they return to their village, are celebrated at a large feast, receive new names, and are expected to become responsible adult members of their society. Passage for the Kaguru girl is not as complex as for boys and occurs when she experiences her first menstruation and is taught the ways of womanhood by her grandmother or older women in the tribe.

Tikopia

The Tikopia is a Polynesian culture in Melanesia. The ritual is initiated when the boy participates in a Nataki ramanga (torch fishing expedition) with other men in community. The day after, the young boy's cheeks, neck, and chest are rubbed with tumeric. The major event is the circumcision. Large quantities of food are stored up and the boy is anointed with turmeric continuously prior to the circumcision. The mother's brother (tuatina) performs the procedure. After the ceremony, the family sings mourning songs. As the boy enters the house, he is greeted by his father. This is followed by a lavish exchange of gifts and an elaborate meal. After the meal, the boy is taken into the forest by the uncle and taught to care for his penis. The healing takes about a month. When the healing is complete, the boy is considered an adult. Tikopian culture is relatively neglectful of a female puberty ritual.

!Kung

The !Kung are a tribe in the Kalahara desert. There are separate and different rituals for boys and for girls. For the boy initiate, the first ceremony is when the men and boys in the group go away and dance for several days and nights. Afterward, the boy initiate has a line incised on his forehead and his hair is cut. The major event is he must kill two large animals (one male, and one female) before he can take a wife. He is prepared for these events by accompanying his father on hunts. When the Rite of the Kill (killing of the large animals) has occurred and the boy is successful, cuts are made in his chest, back, and arms, and fat from the animal is rubbed in. Although the preparation for the killing begins at age 12, the necessary kills occur between ages 15 and 18. The boy may then take a wife. For girls, the ritual begins with the first menstruation. She is carried by an old woman to an isolated shelter. The old woman stays with her. Women and men in the village sing the first menstruation music. When the menstruation has stopped, a design is painted on the girl's face. The girl leaves the shelter and resumes her activities. The final ceremony occurs during the first time the girl eats or drinks after isolation. An older woman must scrape root into the watering hole and prepare and eat the food with the girl.

Discussion Questions

1)   Why do you think nonwestern cultures have such clear puberty rites of passage?

2)   Why do you think western cultures do not have clear puberty rites of passage?

3) Can you think of some informal activities that mark the transition to adulthood in our culture?

References

Delaney, C. H. 1995. Rites of passage in adolescence. *Adolescence* 30: 891–897.

Fried, M. N., and Fried, M. 1980. *Transition: Four rituals in eight cultures*. New York: W. W. Norton.

Gardiner, H. W., Mutter, J. D., and Kosmitzki, C. 1998. *Lives across cultures: Cross-cultural human development*. Needham Heights, MA: Allyn & Bacon.

Weisfeld, G. 1997. Puberty rites as clues to the nature of human adolescence. *Cross-Cultural Research* 31: 27–54.

Activity

17 _Adulthood Stages_

Concept and Goal

By interviewing two middle-aged adults, one Caucasian-American and one minority (African-American, Latin-American, Asian-American, or Native American), and then discussing the results, you gain a better psychological understanding of adulthood. Also, you are encouraged to examine the similarities and differences between adults of different cultures in their development. You should complete the two interviews individually. Then divide into small-groups and prepare a summary of the interview findings. Each group should present the interview findings to the class and prepare the discussion questions for class interaction.

Instructions

Middle adulthood is defined as being between ages 40 and 60. Select two middle-aged adults to interview. One adult should be Caucasian-American and one should be minority (African-American, Latin-American, Asian-American, or Native American). Inform your two subjects that you might be asking some personal questions, and tell them that you need written informed consent before the interview. The consent form must specify that the participant's identity will remain confidential and that the subject may withdraw from the interview at any time.

You are to make up your own specific questions, but the questions must deal with the following issues.

(1) Participants should be asked about issues in their young adulthood (ages 20–40). Topics might include mate selection and marriage, identity and intimacy, career selection, children and family, the role of the husband and wife in the marriage, and any other questions that you might deem relevant to this stage.

(2) Develop questions regarding issues in middle age (ages 40–60). These may include midlife crisis and empty-nest syndrome, health and mental status, generativity versus stagnation, caring for children and elderly parents, whether middle-age seems to be a time of crisis or time of satisfaction, marriage and family issues, whether the role of the husband and wife in the family has changed, the hypothesis that people become more tuned into their inner lives in middle age, and other relevant topics.

(3) Ask some general questions, such as which period of development (childhood, adolescence, young adulthood, or middle adulthood) has been the best psychologically and why; the issues of whether adolescence is more of a period of "storm and stress" than other stages of development; and any other insights or advice that the subject would like to give you.

(4) Ask some ethnically-related questions of the minority interviewee. What are some issues that must be faced as a minority person in this country? What issues related to your ethnicity have you faced as an adolescent? As a young adult? As a middle-aged adult?

After you have completed your interviews, you will be divided into groups of approximately five students. Group members should share with each other the results of the interviews. In particular, draw conclusions about the extent to which the interview data supports the various theories about adult development (Erik Erikson, Daniel Levinson, George Vaillant, Roger Gould). Also, indicate how minority group persons develop in similar ways to nonminority persons and how minority group persons develop differently from nonminority persons.

Your instructor may also assign a written paper based on this project.

Discussion Questions

1) How did the results of the interviews support various theories of adult development?

2) How did the results of the interviews not support various theories of adult development?

3) How were the Caucasian (nonminority) and minority adults similar in their development?

4) How were the Caucasian (nonminority) and minority adults different in their development?

References

Cavanaugh, J. C. 1997. *Adult development and aging.* 6th ed. Pacific Grove, CA: Brooks Cole.

Erikson, E. H. 1968. Generativity and ego identity. In B. L. Neugarten (ed.), *Middle Age and Aging,* 85–87. Chicago: University of Chicago Press.

Moeller, T. G. 1987. Stages and issues in adult development. In V. P. Makosky, L. G. Whittenmore, and A. M. Rogers (eds.), *Activities Handbook for the Teaching of Psychology* (Vol. 2). Washington, DC: American Psychological Association.

Stereotypes about the Elderly

Concept and Goal

This activity demonstrates the false myths that our society has about the elderly. This activity also shows how many "isms" are based on negative stereotypes and can lead to discrimination against the groups involved. This is a small-group activity. In your group, you should counter each ageism presented. Each small-group should present the responses and the discussion questions for class interaction.

Instructions

Stereotypes are oversimplified and biased views about a group of people. Katz and Braly (1933) and Gilbert (1951) indicate the stereotypes associated with various racial/ethnic groups. American college students were in agreement as rating Chinese as superstitious (34%) and sly (29%), English as sportsmanlike (53%) and intelligent (46%), Germans as scientifically-minded (78%) and industrious (65%), Irish as pugnacious (45%) and quick-tempered (39%), Italians as artistic (53%) and impulsive (44%), Japanese as intelligent (45%) and industrious (43%), Jews as shrewd (79%) and mercenary (49%), and Negroes as superstitious (84%) and lazy (75%). In addition to stereotypes about various ethnic groups, there are stereotypes about the elderly. The stereotypes associated with the elderly are examples of ageism. Below are ten ageisms. Present evidence from your introduction to psychology textbook to counter these ageisms.

1)   Old people are not very interested in sex.

Counter:

2)   Old people should reduce the number of their activities and friendships.

Counter:

3) Intelligence peaks around the age of twenty or thirty and then declines steadily.

Counter:

4) Old dogs can't learn new tricks.

Counter:

5) With all their intellectual deficits, old people don't benefit much from education.

Counter:

6) Elderly patients do not respond well to surgery.

Counter:

7)   After sixty-five, the majority of people are unhealthy.

Counter:

8)   Most old people become senile sooner or later.

Counter:

9)   Most people over sixty-five are financially insecure.

Counter:

10)   Menopause often results in nervous breakdowns.

Counter:

Discussion Questions

1) Why do you think that we create negative stereotypes of the elderly in our society? How might these stereotypes affect our treatment of the elderly?

2) Why did this activity present stereotypes associated with various racial/ethnic groups prior to discussing stereotypes associated with the elderly? Are there similarities? Explain.

3) Can you think of other groups that we tend to negatively stereotype? If so, explain.

References

Gilbert, G. 1951. Stereotype persistence and change among college students. *Journal of Abnormal and Social Psychology* 46: 245–254.

Katz, D. and Braley, K. 1933. Racial stereotypes of one hundred college students. *Journal of Abnormal and Social Psychology* 28: 280–290.

Matlin, M. 1999. *Psychology.* 3rd ed. Fort Worth, TX: Harcourt Brace.

Myers, D. 1998. *Psychology.* 5th ed. New York: Worth.

Schaie, K., and Willis, S. 1986. *Adult development and aging.* 2nd ed. Boston, MA: Little Brown & Co.

Wood, S., and Wood, E. 1999. *The world of psychology.* 3rd ed. Boston, MA: Allyn & Bacon.

Rape as Classical Conditioning

Concept and Goal

This activity demonstrates how a single powerful event, such as rape, can be traumatizing and can lead to a life of conditioned fear; it serves as an example of classical conditioning. This is an individual student activity. Read the passage and complete the activity. The class can then discuss the results and the discussion questions.

Instructions

Read the following passage of a fictional woman who was raped. Then complete the activity at the end of the passage.

A Case of Rape

A woman who lives in the suburbs goes downtown one night to meet friends for dinner at an Italian restaurant. After the dinner, she and her friends say good-bye. She goes to the parking garage alone. As she turns the key to unlock her car, an intruder with a gun forces himself into the car with her. He forces her to drive to a desolate place downtown near a stadium where he repeatedly rapes her. Afterward, he steals her money and valuables, ties her up, and leaves her in the car. For many months, the woman has nightmares about the rape, is afraid of the dark, is afraid to go near her car, and is afraid to go downtown. When she passes by an Italian restaurant, a parking garage, or a stadium, her heart pounds and she sweats. She is afraid of strangers, especially men, who resemble the attacker. Ten years later, the woman's conditioned fears are subsiding. Still, she remains extremely cautious about personal safety and occasionally has nightmares about the experience.

In this scenario, the woman's fear (conditioned response—CR), is powerfully associated with (and generalized to) several locations and people (conditioned stimuli—CS), associated with the rape. List seven conditioned and generalized conditioned stimuli mentioned in the passage.

1. _____

2. _____

3. _____

4. _____

5. _____

6. _____

7. _____

Discussion Questions

1) Can you think of other powerful events, similar to the rape scenario, that are examples of classical conditioning?

2) According to Ivan Pavlov's principles of classical conditioning, what can be done to extinguish the fear that the woman (in the passage) is associating and generalizing to the locations and people you have mentioned?

References

Myers, D. G. 1998. *Psychology.* 5th ed. New York: Worth Publishers.

Walden Two

Concept and Goal

This activity examines two communities, one in Mexico and one in the United States, that apply the operant conditioning principles of B. F. Skinner. You should read the passage and then prepare the discussion questions for class interaction.

Instructions

Read the following passage from Bolt's *Instructor's Manual* to accompany Myer's *Psychology*, 5th edition (1998) and answer the discussion questions.

Walden Two

B. F. Skinner, in his book, *Walden Two* (1948), describes an ideal community based on his principles of operant conditioning. This community is a utopia; the community has no major social problems such as crime, racism, unemployment, or poverty. Petty jealousies, boredom, and laziness have been eliminated. One of Walden Two's most attractive features is a labor credit system. With this system, labor credits replace currency as payment for work performed. Residents are not charged for goods or services, but each agrees to contribute 1200 labor credits per year. Unpleasant work has a higher credit value, and thus is not performed over long periods. Residents work an average of 28 hours a week.

In Walden Two, the residents share property in common, enjoy a high standard of living, and spend their leisure time playing chess or painting. Child care is communal and in the hands of child-rearing experts. The nuclear family does not exist. Ethical and moral conditioning is complete by age 6 and principles of reinforcement (positive, negative, and punishment) are systemically applied in the socialization of the child. For example, partial reinforcement is used to develop frustration tolerance. Beginning at 6 months of age, babies are given toys designed to develop perseverance. In order for a toy to be reinforcing, say, for a music box to play, the infant learns to pull a ring. When the infant has learned to respond, the reward is delivered on a variable-ratio schedule. Without experiencing great frustration, very young children begin to build up perseverance that serves them well later in life.

Another significant aspect of Walden Two life is the use lollipops to teach self-control. Every morning preschoolers are given suckers that have been dipped in powdered sugar so that a single lick can be detected. The children may eat the candy in the afternoon only if they can keep from licking it in the meantime. The child who takes a small, immediate reward sacrifices the larger, delayed reward of a whole lollipop.

While Walden Two has its own code of behavior, there is little institutionalized government. Neither a democracy nor a totalitarian state, the community is run by a six-member Board of Planners. Managers are in charge of child care, agriculture, public relations, etc. Visitors are welcome, but, like residents, must work for their keep. Walden Two is composed of about 1000 members and has sister communities elsewhere.

Although Walden Two is a fictional community developed by B. F. Skinner, a few communities have in reality been developed based on the Walden Two blueprint. Los Horcones, an outpost community in Mexico's Sonora Desert founded in the late 1960s, is a good example. Also, Twin Oaks, a small community also founded in the late 1960s near Richmond, Virginia, is another example; Twin Oaks prefers the term "intentional community." Both communities are still in existence.

The residents of Los Horcones have attempted to live by the simple statement on the welcome sign at the edge of their land: "We apply the science of behavior to the design of a new society." The community was established when Juan Robinson, a university psychology student in Mexico City, read *Walden Two* and became a convert. After he and his wife had successfully applied Skinner's principles to the treatment of retarded children, along with four urban friends, they moved to the countryside to establish Los Horcones. They first outlined the details of what they considered a collective lifestyle in the form of a Code of Adult Behavior. The adults were to be parents to all children, residents would be discouraged from saying "mine" and encouraged to say "ours," and casual sex would be strongly discouraged. Los Horcones was to be a living experiment, a cultural lab, in which they could test Skinner's ideas. The Robinsons would be the researchers but also, together with the children, the pigeons.

At latest report, Los Horcones has a population of 26 adults and children. The community farms and is 75 percent self-sufficient in terms of the food it needs, buying only such staples as rice and flour. A small bedroom is the only space an adult can call his or her own. There's a basketball court, a swimming pool called Walden Pond, and one or more wood and metal shops. A dozen or so mentally impaired children are housed in a dormitory which earns enough to buy supplies. A pigeon lab is used for behavioral experiments. Thus far, the community has published 20 papers in academic journals; these papers examine, among other things, the steps Los Horcones has taken to achieve a system of government by consensus and the kinds of reinforcers that have seemed most effective in producing behavioral change. One research topic has been whether children can learn to postpone reinforcement. Using M & M's, the coordinator of childcare tells the 2 through 7 year-olds that "You can eat it now, but if you wait until I say "eat" you get another." Results indicate that the children will wait up to four minutes.

In general, the children receive an enormous amount of attention from all the adults, and they are bright, sociable, and seem to feel capable and loved. The community is not without its problems, however. Adults work more than the four hours Skinner projected in Walden Two. In fact, they all work at least eight hours a day, 6-1/2 days a week. And the main problem involves efforts to correct the adults' training in individualistic living. People who have been reared to believe in individuality will often find it difficult to adapt to the philosophy that other people's happiness is their own happiness. Possessiveness and jealousy are hard to eradicate. Many people have left the community voluntarily after finding that they disliked the communal lifestyle. In fact, over the past 20 years, more than 60 people have come and gone.

Twin Oaks is one of the longest-running and largest communes. It is located on 450 acres of farms, fields, and woods. Its present population consists of 87 adults and 13 children who share income and property. The 28-hour week proposed by Skinner hasn't yet proved practical; members work 45 hours weekly. Most of the work requires physical labor, including milking the cow. Initially Twin Oaks attempted to use a modified form of Walden Two's labor credit system—having some form of labor worth more credit than others—but residents found this aspect of the system too divisive and dropped it.

Sources of income include hammock- and tofu-making businesses. The community makes a $600,000 annual profit selling hammocks to the Pier 1 store chain. Unlike many communities that disintegrate over money issues, Twin Oaks obtained its contract with Pier 1 early on, so that its profit grew along with the company. The profits go into a general budget, but each member gets $61 a month in spending money. In addition to making sure that everyone worked, they were specific in their plans that everyone share clothes from a communal clothing room and that children be raised by the whole community. Although some parents were attracted by the later requirement, others have been reluctant to relinquish control and share authority. Over its history, residents have left to form nuclear families not permitted in Twin Oaks. Although three planners have been in charge of the community's overall direction, residents attend open meetings to consider community issues. The entire community gets to vote for and against fundings for each project, whether it is starting a video library or raising chickens and goats. Unlike residents of Walden Two, most members are interested in the community's politics, bringing a strong democratic tradition to Twin Oaks. There is no television at Twin Oaks and the use of VCRs is still being debated.

The community does have what it calls "leaving issues." By far the most frequent of these is a failed romance. Boyfriends and girlfriends break off their relationships and become involved with someone else in the community. From the first, sex was to be an entirely personal matter, but everyone expected it to be less constrained than in mainstream life. Shifting sexual alliances were not to be controlled by the community and that is still the case.

Although Twin Oaks does not follow the principles of Walden Two to the letter, members says they try to apply Skinner's concept of positive reinforcement in everything they do. B. F. Skinner visited the community at least twice before his death. Some years ago he reported that Twin Oaks could very well become something close to Walden Two when it gets bigger.

Discussion Questions
1) How do the two communities, Los Horcones and Twin Oaks, apply B. F. Skinner principles of operant conditioning (positive reinforcement, negative reinforcement, punishment, shaping, extinction)?

2) How are Los Horcones and Twin Oaks similar to Skinner's fictional community, Walden Two? Are are the two communities different from Walden Two?

3) Can you think of cultures that might have a difficult time adjusting to communities such as Los Horcones, Twin Oaks, or Walden Two? Explain your answer. Can you think of cultures that may adjust more readily to communities such as Los Horcones, Twin Oaks, or Walden Two? Explain your answer.

References

Bolt, M. 1998. *Instructor's manual* to accompany Myer's *Psychology*. 5th ed. New York: Worth.

Cordes, C. November 1984. Easing toward perfection at Twin Oaks. *American Psychological Association Monitor,* 30–31.

Fishman S. January/February 1991. The town B. F. Skinner boxed. *Health*, 50–60.

O'Brien, E. October 20, 1996. Is it utopia yet? *The Record*, YT–1,YT–17.

Skinner, B. F. 1948. *Walden two*. New York: Macmillan.

Source: Passage from Bolt, M. 1998. *Instructor's manual* to accompany Myer's *Psychology*. 5th ed., 8: 15–17. New York: Worth Publishers.
From *Instructor's Manual* to Accompany David Myer's *Psychology*, Martin Bolt. Worth Publishers, Inc., New York, 1998. Reproduced with permission.

Concept and Goal

This activity examines the factors that led European Christians to help free Jews from Nazi-occupied Europe. Read the passage and prepare the discussion questions for class interaction.

Instructions

Read the following passage from Bolt's *Instructor's Manual* to accompany Myer's *Psychology*, 5th edition (1998), and answer the discussion questions. This passage examines London's (1970) work on Europeans who risked their lives by helping Jews escape Nazi-occupied Europe, and their personality characteristics. He recorded conversations with 27 rescuers and 42 rescued people, all of whom had emigrated from Europe to the United States since 1945. Oliner and Oliner (1988) also studied altruistic behavior in Nazi Europe.

Observational Learning

London (1970) found that rescuers who remained committed to the cause of rescuing Jews from Nazi-occupied Europe shared three personality characteristics: 1) a spirit of adventurousness, 2) an intense identification with a parental model of moral conduct, and 3) a sense of being socially marginal. The first characteristic is exemplied by a rescuer in the Dutch underground who had a sort of extracurricular hobby of putting sugar in the gas tanks of German army trucks. The second characteristic is apparent in an interview with another German rescuer, who stated, "I came from a poor family ... my mother said to me when we were small ... regardless of what you do with your life be honest. When it comes to the day you have to make a decision, make the right one. It could be a hard one. But even the hard ones should be right ones." Finally, social marginally was typified by yet another rescuer who reported that he had stuttered as a child, and so had always been friendless. While his family was nominally Lutheran, his mother never went to church. His father, however, attended regularly. This was the reverse of the typical German family's religious practices. London suggest that this prior marginality served the rescuer well as he worked in isolation.

Oliner and Oliner (1988) also examined rescuers of Jews in Nazi Europe. They reported that those who rescued Jews were motivated by three primary factors. About 11 percent were motivated primarily by a commitment to the principles of justice. These people had strong beliefs about how others ought to be treated that came from significant others. Fifty-two percent were motivated by social norms. Helping was seen as obligatory by friends, family, or church in offering help. They did what they felt others expected. The remaining 37 percent were moved by empathy, by the suffering of those whose lives were in danger. This group was thus moved by their feelings of connection to the victim.

The passage demonstrates that London and Oliner and Oliner found many reasons that led others to rescue Jews from Nazi Europe. Both authors found that those who risked their lives tended to have a close relationship with at least one parent who modeled a strong moral or humanitarian concern, an example of observational learning.

Discussion Questions

1) Albert Bandura coined the term observational learning, the way in which we observe and imitate other's behaviors. How do London's and Oliner and Oliner's studies demonstrate observational learning? Explain.

2) What other explanations are given for why the rescuers helped the Jews escape Nazi Europe?

3) Can you think of another example of observational learning? If so, describe it.

References

Bolt, M. 1998. *Instructor's manual* to accompany Myer's *Psychology.* 5th ed. New York: Worth.

London, P. 1970. The rescuers: Motivational hypotheses about Christians who saved Jews from the Nazis. In J. Macaulay and L. Berkowitz (eds.), *Altruism and Helping Behavior.* Orlando, FL: Academic Press.

Oliner, S., and Oliner, P. 1988. *The altruistic personality: Rescuers of Jews in Nazi Europe.* New York: Macmillan.

Activity

22

Food Aversions

Concept and Goal

This activity examines whether there are gender differences in food aversions. You should complete the scale individually, but the class should analyze the results of the activity and review the discussion questions.

Instructions

To measure individual and group differences in food aversions, indicate whether you like or dislike the following foods. Indicate L for "Like" and D for "Dislike."

_____ 1. Calves' brains

_____ 2. Celery

_____ 3. Clam dip

_____ 4. Eggs

_____ 5. Hominy

_____ 6. Kidney stew

_____ 7. Lamb

_____ 8. Leftovers

_____ 9. Nuts

_____ 10. Oysters

_____ 11. Tripe

_____ 12. Turtle soup

_____ 13. Waffles

_____ 14. Watermelon

_____ 15. Whole-wheat bread

Your instructor will give you instructions to complete the assignment.

Discussion Questions

1) Research indicates that females have greater food aversions (dislike more foods) than males. Was there a gender difference in the scores for your class that was consistent with existing research? If so, why do you think this occurred? If there was no gender difference, give possible reasons why.

2) How can negative reactions to a food that we eat for the first time possibly be conditioned (that is, create food aversions)?

References

Byrne, D., Golightly, C., and Capaldi, E. 1963. Construction and validation of the food attitude scale. *Journal of Consulting Psychology* 27: 215–222.

Smith, W. I., Powell, E. K., and Ross, S. 1955. Food aversions: Some additional personality correlates. *Journal of Consulting Psychology* 19: 145–149.

23 *Constructive Memory*

Concept and Goal

The rumor chain game provides a dramatic illustration of how information in long-term memory can be distorted during encoding and retrieval by a person's prior knowledge. This is a class activity. After the class has completed the activity, you should prepare the discussion questions for class interaction.

Instructions

The instructor will provide instructions to carry out this activity during class.

Discussion Questions

1) Did the story change with each retelling of the story? If so, how did the story change?

2) Was information added that was not in the original story? If so, explain what kind of information was added.

3) Explain how prior attitudes about gender and race might affect our encoding and recall of information.

4) What is meant by the phrase "memory is constructive?"

References

Bartlett, F. C. 1932. *Remembering: A study in experimental and social psychology.* Cambridge: Cambridge University Press.

Activity

24

Color Labeling

Concept and Goal

This activity encourages you to examine cultural differences in the perception of color. You are exposed to a limited number of color categories. This is a small-group activity. Your group should do the activity and answer the questions for the two handouts. The group should then share the answers and prepare the discussion questions for class interaction.

Materials

Your instructor will provide your group with a set of color chips.

Instructions

The physical properties of color can be defined using three variables (Armstrong, 1991). First is *hue*: the pure colors that can be seen in a rainbow and in the electromagnetic spectrum by passing white light through a prism and can be measured in wavelengths (Lindsay & Norman, 1972). Color can also be classified by *luminosity* (or brightness); for example, a range of pale pink or dark red would constitute a brightness scale. The third variable is *intensity* (or saturation), that is, the degree of freedom from white; for example, pink would have lower saturation than red because of the larger amount of white in it, whereas dark red would have high saturation. All three criteria are used to define color in modern Western societies, but this is not necessarily the case in other societies.

Your instructor will assign you to groups of approximately five students and will give each group a set of color chips. First, classify your color chips into groups containing the eleven basic colors used in the English language (see Handout 1). Second, classify the same color chips using the basic terms available to speakers of Gouro (one of the languages spoken in the Ivory Coast in Africa (see Handout 2). Answer the questions on each handout.

Discussion Questions

1)   Was the classification of the color chips based on Berlin and Kay's eleven color categories or the classification of the color chips based on the Gouro speakers the hardest? Explain your answer.

2)   What does this activity suggest about the influence of culture on color perception?

3)   In the subfield of cognitive psychology is a theory known as the Whorfian hypothesis. This hypothesis states that one's language influences one's perception of the world. The fact that a culture's language contains a limited or a vast number of labels to categorize a phenomenon is a reflection of how limited or how vast distinctions are made in perceiving that phenomenon. How does the idea that culture affects our color perception relate to the Whorfian hypothesis?

References

Gourves-Hayward, A. 1998. Color my world. In T. M. Singelis (ed.), *Teaching about Culture, Ethnicity, & Diversity: Exercises and Planned Activities*. Thousand Oaks, CA: Sage.

Kay, P., and Kempton, W. 1984. What is the Sapir-Whorf hypothesis? *American Anthropologist* 1: 86.

Lindsay, P., and Norman, D. 1972. *Human information processing*. San Diego, CA: Academic Press.

McNeill, N. B. 1972. Colour and colour terminology. *Journal of Linguistics* 8: 21–34.

Sapir, E. 1929. *The status of linguistics as a science in culture, language and personality.* Berkeley: University of California Press.

Handout 1

Take the set of color chips and put them into the following categories.

Basic color terms   *Number on color chip*

1) Black

2) White

3) Red

4) Green

5) Yellow

6) Blue

7) Brown

8) Purple

9) Pink

10) Orange

11) Gray

Compare your findings with the other groups of students and answer the following questions.

1)   Were there any disagreements? If so, where and why?

2)   Did you find the task difficult? Give reasons for your answer.

3)   What names would you use to classify these colors? Compare the names used by the student groups to classify colors with the names given by the paint manufacturer.

Handout 2

Speakers of Gouro, one of the languages spoken in the Ivory Coast, have three basic color terms to classify colors. They are ti—black, fou—white, and son—red. Take the same color chips as before and put them into these three groups.

Gouro   *Number of color chip*

1) Ti

2) Fou

3) Son

As before, compare your group's findings with the other groups of students and answer the following questions.

1) Were there any disagreements? If so, where and why?

2) How did you go about this task?

3) Did you find it more difficult than the last activity? Give reasons for your answer.

4) Did the number of terms available to you change the way you perceived the colors? Explain.

5) What difficulties might you have in your culture if you only had these three color terms?

Activity

25 — *Cognitive Maps*

Concept and Goal

This activity examines how culture shapes our cognitive maps, our perception of our physical and spatial environments. This is a small-group activity. Each student in the group should draw a map. The group should then analyze the maps drawn. Finally, the group should prepare a discussion of the findings of similarities and differences among the maps for the class and the group should prepare the discussion questions for class interaction.

Instructions

Cognitive psychologists have long been interested in the navigational patterns of humans; this is termed cognitive mapping. We use two types of knowledge in our effort to learn about the spatial world: route knowledge and survey knowledge. Route knowledge is related to the specific pathways used to get between locations. If a stranger on my campus asked me how to find the library, I would say something like "From the entrance to the campus (Frey Road), you take Cobb Avenue to the Lot B parking lot. The Carmichael Student Center and bookstore are to the right of the parking lot, and the library is directly behind the student center and bookstore." In this case, I would be giving the stranger route information. Survey knowledge, on the other hand, deals with more global relationships between environmental cues. I might answer the stranger's questions by saying "It's over there, in that general direction." Another more direct way to form survey knowledge is to study a map. The distortions of memory for geographical locations has been studied. It has been recognized that humans read physical or spatial environments based on individual experiences and cultural backgrounds producing in that person's mind's eye a cognitive site map. That means that a representation of the spatial environment is filtered through an individual's experiences, values, biases, interests, and sense of self.

First, draw a map of the United States and fill in as many states and major cities as possible. After you have drawn your map, the instructor will assign you to a group of five students, and the group should make a list of commonalities and unique items of the individual students' maps. Speculate on what the similarities and the differences mean vis-à-vis backgrounds of the group members.

Second, the class should discuss what you think all the maps reveal about the people who created them. Consider interests, experiences, values, cultures, and issues of power.

Discussion Questions

1) In examining the maps drawn by you and your classmates, what similarities did you see in how the maps were drawn?

2)   What differences did you see in how the maps were drawn?

3)   What do you think the maps reveal about the way different individuals construct a reality of the same place? Were there cultural differences in the construction of the maps? If so, explain the nature of the cultural differences.

4)   Do you think that males and females could differ in their mental maps? Explain.

References

Beaty, W. W., and Troster, A. I. 1987. Gender differences in geographic knowledge. *Sex Roles* 16: 565–590.

Downs, R. M., and Stea, D. 1983. *Image and environment.* New York: Aldine.

Renfro, E., and Hardwick, S. W. 1998. Cognitive site mapping. In T. M. Singelis (ed.), *Teaching about Culture, Ethnicity, and Diversity: Exercises and Planned Activities.* Thousand Oaks, CA: Sage.

Saarinen, T. F., Parton, M., and Billberg, R. 1996. Relative size of continents on world sketch maps. *Cartographica* 33: 37–47.

Solso, R. L. (1988). *Cognitive psychology.* 2nd ed. Boston: Allyn & Bacon.

Activity

26   *Idiom Usage*

Concept and Goal

The activity demonstrates two ideas related to the use of linguistic idioms.

1) Although the same statements (idioms) may be used in different cultures, they can have different meanings (Exercise 1)
2) There are idioms that are specific to a culture that individuals from another culture may not understand (Exercise 2).

This is a small-group activity. Your group should respond to the items for Exercises 1 and 2. The class should then review and discuss the answers and the discussion questions.

Instructions

Complete Exercise 1 based on the culture specified. Next, complete Exercise 2. Exercise 2 presents idioms that are specific to American culture. Idioms are phrases peculiar to a specific culture whose meaning can't be understood from the ordinary meanings of the words in the phrases.

Exercise 1—What Am I Trying to Say?

Briefly define each of the following underlined terms or phrases based on the culture specified.

1. knickers

America:

Britain:

2. "The project will be finished at the end of the day."

America:

Britain:

3. A business indicates that there is a backlog at its warehouse.

America:

Britain:

4. At a meeting, one of the participants suggests <u>tabling the next item</u>.

America:

Britain:

5. A friend of yours tells you that when she meets her boyfriend she will <u>fill him in</u>.

America:

Britain:

6. A friend of yours tells you that his <u>presentation bombed</u>.

America:

Britain:

7. You are visiting someone with your friend and she refers to an older person that is present as her <u>aunt</u>.

America:

West Africa:

Key
1. America: knee-length trousers
Britain: women's underpants

2. America: usually taken literally, that is, that the project will be completed by the end of the working day
Britain: the project will be done when it will be done—finish time is open-ended

3. America: there is a list of orders waiting to be filled
Britain: the warehouse has an overstocked inventory

4. America: put the discussion off until another time
Britain: discuss the item immediately

5. America: that she will elaborate/clarify/tell him
Britain: that she wants to hit the person over the head

6. America: the presentation was a failure
Britain: the presentation was a success

7. America: the person is a relative (sister of either your friend's mother or father)
West Africa: respectful terms of address for any older person (<u>Note:</u> this usage is sometimes used among African-Americans, also)

Exercise 2—What Am I Trying to Say?
Briefly define each of the following underlined terms or phrases. Each of the items is an idiom commonly used in the United States.

1. He has been assigned to the <u>graveyard shift</u>.

2. <u>"How's it going?"</u>

3. <u>Don't make waves.</u>

4. This is a <u>whole new ball game</u>.

5. He is a <u>backseat driver</u>.

6. It is <u>raining cats and dogs</u>.

7. <u>"What's up?"</u>

8. We are <u>playing for all the marbles</u>.

9. Could you give me <u>a ballpark figure</u> on that?

10. She is putting on a <u>dog and pony show</u>.

Key

1. work during the late night hours.
2. How are you?
3. Don't create any trouble.
4. situation that will be more challenging.
5. person who is not in control giving orders to the person in control.
6. raining very hard.
7. How are you?
8. taking a big risk.
9. numerical estimate.
10. doing an elaborate show or presentation.

Discussion Questions

1)   What items did you have difficulty with in Exercises 1 and 2?

2)   Can you think of idioms in the English language that were not mentioned in Exercise 2?

3)   What do the idioms listed in this activity indicate about persons who are attempting to learn or understand a new language?

References

Axtell, R. E. (ed.). 1993. *Do's and taboos around the world.* 3rd ed. New York: Wiley.

Dresser, N. 1996. *Multicultural manners: New rules of etiquette for a changing society.* New York: Wiley.

Hill, G. W, IV, and Grimes, T. August 1997. *Some resources for teaching cross-cultural & ethnic issues in psychology.* Paper presented at the American Psychological Association meeting,

Chicago, IL.

Jenkins, A. 1995. *Turning corners: The psychology of African-Americans.* Boston: Allyn & Bacon.

Source: Activity by Hill, G.W., IV, and Grimes, T. August 1997. *Some resources for teaching cross-cultural & ethnic issues in psychology.* Paper presented at the American Psychological Association meeting, Chicago, IL. Reprinted with permission of the Office of Teaching Resources in Psychology, Society for the Teacing of Psychology.

Activity

27 _English–Official U.S. Language?_

Concept and Goal

This activity is designed to encourage you to think about whether English should be declared the official U.S. language and the impact such a law would have on bilingual education. This is a small-group activity. Your group should think of as many arguments for and against English-only laws as possible. Each group should then present the arguments and prepare the discussion questions for class interaction.

Instructions

California, noted for its culturally-diverse population, made national news in 1986 by passing a referendum declaring English as its official language. Over the next years, 17 other states followed suit, each proclaiming their desire to protect a common language and culture in the United States. These laws require children who can't speak English or children who are bilingual (speak more than one language) to be taught only English in school. There are supporters and opponents of English-only laws. Think of pro and con arguments for English-only laws.

Discussion Questions

1) Do the pro or con arguments related to English-only laws seem most persuasive to you? Why?

2) What side would you support if you and your children immigrated to this country from another country? Explain.

3) What side would you support if you were a teacher at a school with a large immigrant population? Explain.

References

August, D., and Garcia, E. 1988. *Language minority education in the United States.* Springfield, IL: Charles C. Thomas.

Berk, L. 1997. *Child development.* 4th ed. Needham Heights, MA: Allyn & Bacon.

Cazden, C. 1984. *Effective instructional practices in bilingual education.* Washington, DC: National Institute of Education.

Hakuta, K., and Garcia, E. 1989. Bilingualism and education. *American Psychologist* 44: 374–379.

McGroarty, M. 1992. The societal context of bilingual education. *Educational Researcher* 21: 7–9.

Neier, A. February 1, 1994. Watching rights (the use of official languages). *Nation,* p. 187.

Piatt, B. 1993. *Only English? Law and languge policy in the United States.* Albuquerque: University of New Mexico Press.

Wong-Fillmore, L., Ammon, P., McLaughlin, B., and Ammon, M. 1985. *Learning English through bilingual instruction.* Rosslyn, VA: National Clearinghouse for Bilingual Education.

Activity

28

Creole Language

Concept and Goal

This activity is designed to familiarize you with how creole languages develop. These languages develop when people who speak different languages need to communicate with each other. This activity also familiarizes students with support for the nature side of the language acquisition debate, that humans are innately capable of acquiring a language. You should read the passage and then prepare the discussion questions for class interaction.

Instructions

Read the following passage from Laura Berk's *Child Development,* 4th edition, 1997, and answer the discussion questions.

Creole Languages

Can instances be found in which children develop complex language systems with only minimal language input? If so, this evidence would serve as strong support for Noam Chomsky's idea that humans are born with a biological program for language development.

In a series of studies, it has been reported that deaf preschoolers who had not been taught sign language spontaneously produced a gestural communications system strikingly similar to hearing children's verbal language (Goldin-Meadow & Morford, 1985; Goldin-Meadow & Mylander, 1983). However, critics claim that the deaf children's competencies might have resulted from subtle gestural exchanges with their parents (Bohannon, 1993).

The study of creoles offers an alternative test of the nature perspective. Creoles are languages that arise rapidly from pidgins, which are minimally developed emergency tongues that result when several language communities migrate to the same area and no dominant language exists to support interactions among them. In 1876, large numbers of immigrants from China, Japan, Korea, the Philippines, Puerto Rico, and Portugal came to Hawaii to work in the sugar industry. The multilingual population quickly outnumbered other residents—English speakers and native Hawaiians alike. Out of this melting pot, Hawaiian Pidgin English emerged, a communication system with a small vocabulary and narrow range of grammatical options that permitted new immigrants to get by in everyday life. Pidgin English, however, was so limited in its possibilities and applied so unsystematically that it may have offered young children too little language input from which to learn. Yet within 20 to 30 years, a new complex language, Hawaiian Creole English, which borrowed vocabulary from its pidgin and foreign-language predecessors, became widespread.

Bickerton (1981, 1983, 1990) concludes that the next generation of children must have invented the language, relying on innate mechanisms. There are two types of evidence to support this idea. (1) The structure of creole languages is similar around the world, suggesting a common genetic program underlies them. (2) Creole grammar resembles the linguistic structures children first use when acquiring any language and their incorrect hypotheses about complex grammatical forms. For example, expressions like "he no bite you" and "where he put the toy?" are perfectly correct in Hawaiian Creole English.

Discussion Questions

1) How can the development of pidgin and creole languages facilitate communications among peoples?

2) This passage traces the development of the Hawaiian creole language. Can you cite examples of creole languages that have developed in other geographical areas? What languages were combined to create those creoles?

References

Berk, L. 1997. *Child development.* 4th ed. Needham Heights, MA: Allyn & Bacon.

Bickerton, D. 1990. *Language and species.* Chicago: University of Chicago Press.

Bickerton, D. 1983. Creole languages. *Scientific American* 249: 116–122.

Bickerton, D. 1981. *Roots of language.* Ann Arbor, MI: Karamo.

Bohannon, J. N. 1993. Theoretical approaches to language acquisition. In J. Berko Gleason (ed.), *The Developmental Psychology of Language.* 3rd ed., 239–297. New York: Macmillan.

Goldin-Meadow, S., and Morford, M. 1985. Gesture in early language: Studies of deaf-hearing children. *Merrill-Palmer Quarterly* 31: 145–176.

Goldin-Meadow, S. and Mylander, C. 1983. Gestural communication in deaf children: Non-effect of parental input on language development. *Science* 221: 372–374.

Concept and Goal

This exercise uses folktales to examine how cultures differ in whether their communication is direct or indirect. Folktales are used because they can carry a culture's customs and norms. This is a small-group activity. After individual students in the group have read each story, your group should answer the questions associated with each of the two stories. Each group should then present to the class their responses to questions associated with each story, and prepare the discussion questions for class interaction.

Instructions

Folktales are carriers of culture as well as forms of entertainment (Cargile & Sunwolf, 1998). Cargile and Sunwolf point out that "values, customs, norms, roles, and religious beliefs are often embedded within the narrative of folktales and may be passed on from one generation to the next. The stories of a culture are usually effective tools for socialization of its members, but they can also provide outsiders a glimpse of a culture with which they are not familiar."

According to Cargile and Sunwolf (1998), folktales can be used to indicate the appropriate way to communicate with others. One useful approach to communicating with others involves the direct statement of the self's needs and desires. This mode of communication expects people to be honest and up front about what they have to say and not beat around the bush. A second, and opposite, mode of expression involves indirect communication. According to Searle (1969), indirect communication takes place when the speaker expresses to the hearer more than is actually said; the success of this method of expression depends on the hearer's power of inference. Read the following two folktales and consider multiple answers to the questions pertaining to each story following the tales.

The Lions' Whisker [1]
(adapted and retold by Sunwolf; Cargile & Sunwolf, 1998)

Once there lived a couple who was not quite content in a small village in Ethiopia. The husband showed little interest in the marriage, though they had not been married long. He usually came home late from working in the fields—and sometimes, he failed to come home at all. His wife loved him but felt so ignored by her husband, and felt such hostility from him, that she knew she needed help. She went to talk with the oldest and wisest man in the village.

The old man listened patiently to her bitter words. When he asked her what she had thought of doing, she said that she felt she should probably confront her husband with his duties and with her needs. She would demand better treatment. The wise elder smiled. "That would be one choice, of course," he said softly. "But I know of a potion what will change your husband into an obedient and loving man. If you give it to him, he will come home on time and try always to please you."

"Give it to me. I will pay anything!" she cried. For truly, she wanted to stay married.

"I lack one vital ingredient," continued the wise man. "A single whisker taken from a living lion. If you can bring me such a whisker, I will make the potion and you shall have it."

"I will get it for you," the woman said with determination.

The next day the woman began studying the nearby lions, and she watched them for many days. Finally, she was ready. One day she carried a large chunk of raw meat down to the river where one lion came to drink. Hiding in the forest, she waited quietly until the lion appeared. The woman was frightened. She wanted to run away, but she found the courage to toss the meat to the hungry beast. The lion grabbed the meat, devoured it, and walked slowly back into the jungle.

Every morning that week the women fed the lion in this way, though her fear remained great. During the second week, she came out of her hiding place and let the lion see who was bringing the meat. The third week she moved closer to the lion as he ate, though her body trembled. As time passed, she moved still closer. And when five weeks had passed, she was able to sit down quietly next to the lion while he ate. And so it became possible, one day, for her to gently reach over and plunk a single whisker from his chin.

She ran to the wise man with her prize. He smiled at her in surprise and asked her to explain how she managed to acquire it. After hearing her story, the old man shook his head. "You are brave enough to pull a single whisker from a living lion. This was a dangerous task, which required courage, cleverness, and endless patience. If you can accomplish this, then can you not use that same courage, cleverness, and endless patience to improve your marriage?"

"Take time," he suggested. "By your actions show him your love and your needs, and see what may happen then."

The woman went home and thought about this advice. She never spoke to her husband about her anger or what she had done. But slowly, through her actions and not her words, the relationship began to improve. And one day it came to pass that their marriage had grown into one of intimacy and balance, which lasted for all the years of their lives.

Questions from "The Lion's Whisker" (from Cargile and Sunwolf, 1998):

1) In this story, the husband came home late, if at all. Do you think his behavior was appropriate? Why or why not?

2) Needing help, the woman went to the oldest and wisest man in the village. Do you think elderly persons in our society receive as much respect and attention as this elder did? Should they?

3)   What did the woman learn by feeding the lion? What was the wise man's "potion" for helping the woman's marriage?

4)   What are the advantages and disadvantages of saving the woman's marriage by using what the wise man taught her? Do you think it would work?

5)   What is the "moral" of this story? Do you agree with this moral?

The Woman Who Followed Death [2]

(adapted and retold by Sunwolf; Cargile and Sunwolf, 1998)

Once there lived a young woman who was so loved by her father, and whose wisdom he so respected, that he did the unthinkable: He gave to her the right to choose her own husband, believing only she would know who would be a worthy partner.

Savitri traveled far and listened to many people. She saw a young man with shining eyes guiding and caring for his old blind father. She heard the stories of his virtue. She knew then who should be her partner and she returned to tell her father. Her father's adviser, however, a holy man, was horrified at her choice. "This young man is indeed a person of great value," he admitted, "But it is written that he will die one year from today. Choose another." Savitri trembled, but said, "I have chosen, and whether his life be short or long, I would share it."

For nearly a year the two lived happily. However, on the eve of their anniversary, her husband suddenly dropped to the ground, complaining of a severe headache. Savitri laid him in the shade of a tree, his head on her lap, and watched as her beloved husband's eyes closed and his breathing stopped. Suddenly there appeared a powerful man, his body burned like the sun, though his skin was darker than the deepest night. It was Yama, Lord of Death, come for the spirit of her husband. "Indeed you are full of merit if you can see me, child. Happiness awaits your husband in my kingdom," offered Yama, "He has been a man of great virtue." And with that he pulled the spirit of her husband from his body and turned to leave.

Savitri rose and ran after Yama, and though he moved swiftly, she struggled to follow. She called out, "Lord Yama, though it be your duty to take my husband, yet it is my duty to ask you for his life." The Lord of Death looked puzzled. "No one can ask for a life back once I have taken it. Go home." Yet Savitri followed, knowing firmly what she wanted, and knowing Yama could give it to her if he wished. After many miles Yama turned. "I will not give what you ask—still your directness pleases me. I will grant you a favor—anything but the life of your husband."

Savitri thought quickly. "Please restore to my father-in-law his eyesight." Yama granted this request, but still she followed. "Savitri, you have come far enough."

"Give me the life of my husband," she repeated. Yama shook his head. "No. Still, I admire your devotion and directness. I will grant you another favor—anything but the life of your husband." "Grant many more children to my father," Savitri said. Again, Yama granted her request, but still she followed, scratched and bleeding in her struggle to keep up.

"Savitri, your love must bend to fate. I forbid you to come further. Still, I admire your courage and directness. I will grant you one last favor, but this time ask something for yourself—anything but the life of your husband." Savitri paused.

"Then grant many children to me, and let them be the children of my husband whose soul you have taken!" Yama's red eyes grew wide, and a slow smile spread on his dark face. "Savitri, your wit is as strong as your directness. You have not asked for the life of your husband, yet I cannot grant this wish without returning him to you. You have won your husband's life."

And, indeed thereafter, Savitri and her husband were blessed by a long life together of great peace and harmony—and by many children.

Questions from "The Woman Who Followed Death" (from Cargile & Sunwolf, 1998):

1)   Why was it "unthinkable" that Savitri's father gave her the right to choose her own husband?

2)   The holy man knew that Savitri's choice for a husband would die within a year. Do you believe that our future, or some features of it, may be predetermined?

3) After her husband died, what did Savitri do to get his life back? Did other people in Savitri's position ever do the same thing? (How "normal" was it?) Why or why not?

4) What were the advantages and disadvantages of Savitri's actions?

5) What is the "moral" of this story? Do you agree with this moral?

Discussion Questions

1) What are the advantages and disadvantages of communicating in a direct manner, as Savitri did in "The Woman Who Followed Death?" Can you think of times when you would tell someone exactly what you are thinking?

2) What are the advantages and disadvantages of letting only your actions and gestures speak for you, as the woman in "The Lion's Whisker" did?

3) Can you think of a folktale we may all know that is an example of direct communication? Of indirect communication? List it.

4) Do you think American culture emphasizes direct or indirect communication? Explain.

5) Is folklore itself a direct or indirect method of communication? Explain.

6) Can you find examples of cultural values other than direct/indirect communication that are conveyed in these two folktales? Explain.

End Notes
[1] "The Lion's Whisker," adapted by Sunwolf and used with permission (Cargile & Sunwolf, 1998), is an oral tale and passed on in many similar versions, sometimes involving a tiger.

[2] "The Woman Who Followed Death," adapted by Sunwolf and used with permission (Cargile & Sunwolf, 1998), is one of the best-known tales of India, appears as the tale "Savitri" within "The Mahabharata," India's national epic, and has been passed on orally for centuries.

References
Cargile, A. C., and Sunwolf. 1998. Does the squeaky wheel get the grease? In T. M. Singelis (ed.), *Teaching about Culture, Ethnicity, and Diversity: Exercises and Planned Activities.* Thousand Oaks, CA: Sage.

Gudykunst, W. B., and Ting-Toomey, S. 1988. *Culture and interpersonal communication.* Newbury Park, CA: Sage.

Katriel, T., and Philipson, G. 1981. What we need is communication: Communication as a cultural category in some American speech. *Communication Monographs* 48: 301–317.

Lebra, T. S. 1976. *Japanese patterns of behavior.* Honolulu: University Press of Hawaii.

Searle, J. R. 1969. *Speech acts.* Cambridge, UK: Cambridge University Press.

Activity

30 *Sexist Language*

Concept and Goal

This activity helps you become aware of sexist language, specifically to avoid sexist language and use sex-neutral terms. This is a small-group activity. Your group should indicate why each statement is sexist and provide a nonsexist alternative. Each small-group should then present their responses and prepare the discussion questions for class interacton.

Instructions

The "generic masculine" is the use of masculine pronouns and nouns to refer to all human beings, female and male, instead of males alone. Examples include man, he/his/him, businessman, chairman, forefathers, and mankind. Although it has been asserted that whenever people see or hear masculine pronouns they think of both males and females, research indicates that generic masculine terms are more likely than sex-neutral terms to produce thoughts that are oriented around males and masculinity. For example, potential illustrators for a book are more likely to select all-male photos when the chapter title is Industrial Man or Social Man rather than Industrial Life or Society. Furthermore, Briere and Lanktree (1983) found that students who saw the generic masculine version rated a career in psychology as being less attractive for women than did students who saw sex-neutral versions.

Exercise 1

The following are sexist terms. Indicate why these terms are sexist and provide nonsexist alternatives to these terms.

1. mankind:

2. manhole cover:

3. the average man:

4. manpower:

5. four-man team:

6. woman doctor:

7. stewardess:

8. mothering:

9. businessman:

10. fireman:

11. foreman:

12. policeman:

13. chairman:

14. sportsmanship:

15. bachelor's degree:

Exercise 2

The following are sexist statements. Indicate why these statements are sexist and provide nonsexist alternatives to these terms.

1. The client is usually the best judge of the value of his counseling.

2. Participants were 19–21-year-olds who were attending a girl's school.

3. The authors acknowledge the assistance of Mrs. John Smith.

4. Men and women, sons and daughters, boys and girls, and husbands and wives.

5. Men and girls were in attendance.

6. Research scientists often neglect their wives and children.

7. Only freshmen were eligible for the study.

8. The girls in the office greeted all clients.

Discussion Questions

1) This activity indicates that language can be sexist. Can language be ethnically biased? If so, give examples.

2) What may be the impact if nonsexist language is used in textbooks?

References

Briere, J., and Lanktree, C. 1983. Sex-role related effects of sex bias in language. *Sex Roles* 9: 625–632.

Cronin, C., and Jreisat, S. 1995. Effects of modeling on the use of nonsexist language among high school freshpersons and seniors. *Sex Roles* 33: 819–830.

McMinn, M. R., Lindsay, S. F., Hannun, L. E., and Troyer, P. K.1990. Does sexist language reflect personal characteristics? *Sex Roles* 23: 389–396.

Paludi, M. A. 1990. Nonsexist language usage. In V. P. Makosky, C. C. Sileo, L. G. Whittemore, C. P. Landry, and M. L. Shutley (eds.), *Activities Handbook for the Teaching of Psychology* (Vol. 3). Washington, DC: American Psychological Association.

Publication manual of the American Psychological Association. 3rd ed. 1983. Washington, DC: American Psychological Association.

Activity
31
Developing an IQ Test

Concept and Goal

This activity encourages you to think about how intelligence tests reflect cultural themes and biases. It also encourages you to analyze how intelligence might be defined, how it is likely to operate, how it might be measured, and for what purpose it might be measured, while divorcing you from the particular manner in which intelligence is tested in your own culture. This is a small-group activity. In your group, you are to develop an IQ test and justify it. Each small-group will then present the test developed, the justification for the test, and prepare the discussion questions for class interaction.

Instructions

Your instructor will assign you to a group of about five students. Your group will either choose one of the three cultures below or your instructor will assign you one of the three cultures. Devise an intelligence test for people in that culture; make sure your test includes nonverbal items. Assume that the only people who will use the test results are those in the culture described. Be as specific and detailed as you can. Be ready to discuss the reasons for your choices and state how you think the test should be used within that culture. How would you present your proposed test to people in this culture, and how would they be likely to respond? If you have to convince them to adopt your test, what would you say? Why?

Culture 1

Antarea is a sun-drenched, tropical island nation in the South Pacific, consisting of a series of tiny, closely packed islands. Each island is separated from its neighbor by a thin strip of navigable water, with rivers and streams criss-crossing each island as well. Thus, the primary mode of daily Antarean transportation is swimming. In fact, people commonly spend many hours each day in the water, either going from one place to another or even standing in shallow water to socialize or conduct business transactions. Antareans are completely insulated, never having made contact with any cultures from the rest of the world. Indeed, they are apparently unaware that there even is a "rest" of the world, since no Anterean has ever left the island chain or seen evidence of humans living outside their culture.

Culture 2

Zostereans are people born with a specific brain defect whose only consequence is to prevent the capacity to use speech. They cannot produce speech or understand the speech of others; these characteristics apply to vocal speech, written language, and sign language. Other than this one feature, Zostereans are completely normal. But, because Western cultures emphasize language so heavily, Zostereans find it difficult, confusing, and embarrassing to operate in most Western cultures. Thus, they generally live in their homeland, Zosteria, which is entirely populated by Zostereans, and rarely venture outside its borders.

Culture 3

A magical genie grants Hilda, the historian, one wish. Hilda, says, "Well, I've always wanted to know more about the people who lived on the Earth 4,000 years ago, so bring me some people from that time so I can talk to them." Unfortunately, the genie misunderstood and brought every single human who was alive on Earth exactly 4,000 years ago to the present. Suddenly, millions of these people appeared on the earth mainly in and around the Portland, Oregon area, where Hilda had met the genie. These "Transplantons," as they came to be called by the news media covering this phenomenon, are people who suddenly appeared in the American Pacific Northwest around the turn of the twenty-first century; from the Transplantons' point of view, however, moments ago they were in the time period of 4,000 years ago.

Discussion Questions

1) What factors did you consider important in developing an IQ test for the culture you chose? Why were those factors important?

2) Do you have confidence that the final IQ test you developed will be a reliable and valid measure of intelligence for the cultural group you chose for the purposes you will be administering it? Why or why not?

3) Is it possible to develop a culturally unbiased IQ test? Why or why not?

References

Cole, M., Gay, J., Glick, J., and Sharp, D. 1971. *The cultural context of learning and thinking: An exploration in experimental anthropology.* New York: Basic Books.

Shenker, J., Goss, S., and Bernstein, D. 1997. *Instructor's manual* to accompany Bernstein *Psychology.* 4th ed. Boston, MA: Houghton Mifflin.

Sternberg, R. 1995. Testing common sense. *American Psychologist* 50: 912–927.

Sternberg, R. 1998. *In search of the human mind.* 2nd ed. Forth Worth, TX: Harcourt Brace.

Activity

32

Biased IQ Testing

Concept and Goal

This activity demonstrates the bias that occurred in the testing of immigrants and minorities throughout much of the history of the United States. You should read the passage and then prepare the discussion questions for class interaction.

Instructions

Read the following passage from Conrad and Rafter's *Instructor's Resource Kit* to Accompany Wade and Tavris' *Psychology*, 3rd edition (1993), and answer the discussion questions.

Is the Idea that Race and IQ are Linked a New Idea?

The belief that intelligence is determined by one's ethnicity or race is a modern-day version of earlier theories of nativism. Published in 1875, Richard Dugdale's investigation of the inherited basis of crime, pauperism, disease, and insanity was accepted throughout the world as the best documented evidence of the bad seed, or nativist, theory of evil. In his extensive analysis of the Jukes clan, Dugdale identified over 700 people belonging to the Jukes blood of whom more than 500 were social degenerates. There were those who were immoral, harlots, lecherous, paupers, drunkards, lazy, and fornicators, as well as murderers, rapists, and thieves. So evil and corrupt was this family line that during the 73 years of its studied existence, it cost the taxpayers of New York State over a million dollars.

In 1912, another researcher, Henry Goddard, found further support for the nativist position when he came upon a natural experiment in breeding. A Revolutionary War soldier, whom Goddard dubbed Kallikak (from the Greek kalos, good, and kakos, bad), sired two families, one illegitimate and one legitimate. His first alliance was with a tavern maid who was reportedly mentally defective; he later married a young woman of better stock. What were the consequences of these different unions? Only a few of the nearly 500 descendants from Martin Kallikak's legal marriage could be classified as undesirable. In contrast, the son born of Martin's affair with the tavern maid produced a long line of defective descendants. Of 480 traced descendants, 14 were reported to be feeble-minded, 33 were sexually immoral, 24 were alcoholics, many died in infancy, and others were criminals, brothel keepers and the like.

These studies led some criminologists to accept the theory that social disease, as well as insanity and idiocy, could be inherited. The apparent inevitability that a tainted individual would pass the bad seed onto future generations was a powerful stimulus to the eugenics movement in America. Twenty-seven states proceeded to adopt compulsory sterilization laws to prevent the transmission of such unalterable defects.

Goddard's own eminence rose as a consequence of this famous study, and he was invited by the U.S. Public Service to test the intelligence of European immigrants arriving at New York's Ellis Island. Based on what he described in his

1913 report of testing of the great mass of average immigrants, Goddard claimed to have discovered the following percentages of feeble-minded individuals among them:

Russians	87 percent
Jews	83 percent
Hungarians	80 percent
Italians	79 percent

In 1917, Goddard was able to report a vast increase in deportation of immigrants whose feeble-mindedness was detected by the use of tests of mental ability. (These tests of mental ability were given in English to non-English-speaking people.)

Lewis Terman furthered the idea that those identified as feeble-minded by IQ tests were a menace to society. Terman is well known among psychologists for two contributions: his introduction into the United States in 1916 of a version of the IQ tests developed by French psychologist Alfred Binet, and his longitudinal study of the development of a group of children classified as geniuses on that Stanford Binet IQ test. (Terman was then a professor at Stanford University.) What is less well known is Terman's belief that feeble-mindedness represented a serious menace to society. Terman (1917) wrote: "Only recently have we begun to recognize how serious a menace it is to the social, economic, and moral welfare of the state … If we would preserve our state for a class of people worthy to possess it, we must prevent, as far as possible, the propagation of mental degenerates" (pp. 161, 165). After having found low IQ scores for a pair of Mexican and Indian children he tested, Terman (1916) generalized: "Their dullness seems to be racial, or at least inherent in the family stocks from which they come. The fact that one meets this type with such extraordinary frequency among Indians, Mexicans, Negroes suggests quite forcibly that the whole question of racial differences in mental traits will have to be taken up anew … Children of this group should be segregated in special classes … They cannot master abstractions, but they can often be made efficient workers" (pp. 91–92).

Consider the sources of bias in this evidence.
1) No one would dispute the fact that eminence as recognized social status runs in certain families—but is that support for inheritance or for the social, political, and economic contacts that eminent parents can provide for their offspring? Can we rule out the availability of advantageous social influences, supportive family environments, appropriate role models, and educational opportunities?
2) How was it possible to construct the genetic family trees of the Jukes or Kallikaks from a period of history when public record keeping of vital statistics was rare or incomplete—and did not exist for illegitimate births?
3) How objective are the stigmatizing labels applied by the researchers to the bad-seed offspring: immoral, lazy, perverted? Is fornication an indicator of pathology?

4) How were the tests given to the eastern and southern European immigrants? Were the people, fatigued from months aboard a ship, not allowed to enter the city until they completed the test? In what language were the tests given? One must wonder about the objectivity of the criteria used to assign the categorical label feebleminded when the results included the vast majority of eastern and southern European immigrants.

Clearly, this is one area of research where the personal values of researchers interfered with proper utilization of the scientific method of collecting unbiased data and drawing valid conclusions from reliable data.

Discussion Questions

1) Why do you think that bias has occurred in the intelligence testing of immigrants and minorities throughout much of U.S. history?

2) What do you think can be done to overcome this bias when testing the intelligence of immigrants and minorities?

3) What have your learned from this activity of tracing the history of intelligence testing in the United States?

References

Conrad, E., and Rafter, M. 1993. *Instructor's resource kit* to accompany Wade and Tavris's *Psychology*. 3rd ed. New York: Harper Collins.

Herrnstein, R., and Murray, C. 1994. *The bell curve: Intelligence and class structure in American life*. New York: Free Press.

Jensen, A. 1969. How much can we boost IQ and scholastic achievement? *Harvard Educational Review* 39: 1–23.

Terman, L. 1916. *The measurement of intelligence*. Boston: Houghton Mifflin.

Terman, L. 1917. The intelligence quotient of Francis Galton in childhood. *American Journal of Psychology* 28: 204–215.

Activity

33

Mock IQ Tests

Concept and Goal

In this activity you are exposed to the importance of good validity for an intelligence test; also, you are encouraged to discuss how scores on intelligence tests affect success in life. You should complete the test. After you have scored your test and you have been debriefed, you should prepare the discussion questions for class interaction.

Instructions

Your instructor will give you instructions for the following test of mental ability, the Stevenson Mental Inventory. After your instructor has given you the appropriate instructions, complete the test.

1. The 21st president of the United States was

    a) James A. Garfield.
    b) Rutherford B. Hayes.
    c) Grover Cleveland.
    d) Chester A. Arthur.

2. How many days are in a leap year?

3. What is the Roman numeral expression for 900?

4. In linear measurement, how many rods are in a furlong?

5. What is the best definition of "salubrious"?

    a) wet or slippery
    b) tricky or deceptive
    c) easily fooled
    d) health-giving

6. Which of the following two cities are separated from each other by about the same distance as that which separates New York City and Miami, Florida?

    a) Portland, Oregon, and Los Angeles, California
    b) Phoenix, Arizona, and Salt Lake City, Utah
    c) Chicago, Illinois, and Atlanta, Georgia
    d) Kansas City, Missouri, and Cleveland, Ohio

7. What is 4 percent of 500?

8. Which of the following sentences is grammatically incorrect?

    a) The story is told in a convincing manner.
    b) I drive fast and sometimes careless.
    c) Along the water's edge there are found many wild flowers.
    d) The council has ordered his arrest.

9. If x = 4 and y = 3, then what is x(x - y)?

10. Which of the following was not an order in classical Greek architecture?

    a) doric
    b) gothic
    c) ionic
    d) corinthian

11. "Don't cry over spilled milk" means

    a) avoid being emotional
    b) take good care of your food
    c) do not worry about old mistakes
    d) work in a hurry

12. What is the chemical abbreviation for the element silver?

13. Which of the following words does not belong?

    thicket, beluga, foliage, bough

14. What number comes next in this series?

    1, 3, 5, 7, 11, 13, ___

15. Which of the following animals is not a species of bird?

    a) crappie
    b) canary
    c) condor
    d) finch

16. Which of the following is the northernmost city?

    a) New York, United States of America
    b) Berlin, Germany
    c) Tokyo, Japan
    d) Cairo, Egypt

17. Which of the following is a bone found in the foot?

    a) scaphoid bone
    b) cuboid bone
    c) capitate bone
    d) zygomatic bone

18. BOOK is to INK as RADIO is to

    a) hearing.
    b) sound.
    c) pitch.
    d) dial.

19. What is a harmonica most often used for?

20. Complete the analogy by writing a word ending with the letter shown.

    COUNTRY is to BORDER as BANK is to _ _ _ _ R.

After you have completed the test, your instructor will give you instructions to complete the activity.

Discussion Questions
1) Do you think your intelligence has been accurately measured by this test? Why or why not?

2) What test items seemed most valid as measures of intelligence, and what items seemed least valid?

3) Are there any ways in which this test might be improved?

4) What information would this test give to schools, employers, or leaders of government?

5) How should one interpret the results of the test?

6) Was there any cultural bias in the test? If so, explain. What would be an appropriate alternative?

References

    Aero, R., and Weiner, E. 1983. *IQ test: The brain game.* New York: Quill.

    Shenker, J., Goss, S., and Bernstein, D. 1997. *Instructor's manual* to accompany Bernstein's *Psychology.* 4th ed. Boston, MA: Houghton Mifflin.

Activity

34

Career Aspirations

Concept and Goal

This activity demonstrates how sex stereotyping can occur in hiring employees for jobs, and it demonstrates how resumes can be used to overcome some of the sex-stereotyping that occurs for job applicants. Students will individually have adults rate the resumes they have developed. The class will then analyze the results and review the discussion questions.

Instructions

You will prepare two resumes for a specific position. One of the resumes will be based on the general information provided on the resume worksheet and will not contain stereotype-countering information. The second resume will contain the same general information provided on the resume worksheet but will also contain information countering female myths (stereotype-countering). Develop the two resumes and make two copies of each. One copy of the stereotype-countering resume should include a male applicant's name, while the second copy should include a female applicant's name. Similarly, the nonstereotype-countering resume should include a male applicant's name, while the second copy should include a female applicant's name. Distribute the four resumes to a group of adults and ask them to rate the quality of the resume on a scale from 1 (poor) to 10 (excellent). Each adult should receive one of the four resumes. Your instructor will give you instructions to complete the activity.

Discussion Questions

1) Were the persons whose resumes contained stereotype-countering information or the persons whose resumes did not contain stereotype-countering information rated as the better applicants?

2) Were the males or females rated as having the better resumes?

3) When a female had stereotype-countering information on her resume, was she rated more positively? Why or why not? Did the stereotype-countering information help the males? Why or why not?

References

Berk, L. E. 1997. *Child development.* 4th ed., 513. Needham Heights, MA: Allyn & Bacon.

Glick, P., Zion, C., and Nelson, C. 1988. What mediates sex discrimination in hiring decisions? *Journal of Personality and Social Psychology* 55: 178–186.

Morgan, S., Schor, S., and Martin, L. 1993. Gender differences in career paths in banking. *The Career Development Quarterly* 41: 375–382.

Rukeyser, L., Cooney, J., and Winslow, W. 1988. *Louis Rukeyser's business almanac.* New York: Simon & Schuster.

U.S. Bureau of the Census. 1995. *Statistical abstract of the United States.* 115th ed. Washington, D.C.: U.S. Government Printing Office.

Resume Worksheet

Basic Information

Desired Position:
> Bank Branch Manager

Work Experience:
> 1) Loan Officer, Security National Bank, Washington, D.C., October 1994 to the present
> 2) Teller, Chemical National Bank, Washington, D.C., June 1990 to October 1994

Education:
> B.S., Baldwin College, Business Administration degree

Interests:
> Travel, reading, gardening

Stereotyping-Countering Information (Include a section on the resume titled Work Philosophy and include each of the following four <u>responses</u> in this section.)

Myth 1: Female employees simply want a 9–5 job and are not willing to work extra hours for their careers.

> *Response:* indicate willingness to work extended hours and travel to meetings.

Myth 2: Female employees do not have good leadership skills.

> *Response:* indicate ability to lead others.

Myth 3: Female managers are not as accessible to employees as males.

> *Response:* indicate style of encouraging employees to communicate openly and of getting into the workplace with employees.

Myth 4: Females are more emotional and less logical in decision-making than males.

> *Response:* make a point of having excelled in research methods and statistics courses, logic and decision-making courses, and stress being a logical decision-maker.

Data Worksheet

Female applicant—nonstereotype-countering information

        Participant 1— rating of applicant _____

        Participant 2—rating of applicant _____

        Participant 3—rating of applicant _____

        Participant 4—rating of applicant _____

Female applicant—stereotype-countering information

        Participant 5—rating of applicant _____

        Participant 6—rating of applicant _____

        Participant 7—rating of applicant _____

        Participant 8—rating of applicant _____

Male applicant—nonstereotype-countering information

        Participant 9—rating of applicant _____

        Participant 10—rating of applicant _____

        Participant 11—rating of applicant _____

        Participant 12—rating of applicant _____

Male applicant—stereotype-countering information

        Participant 13—rating of applicant _____

        Participant 14—rating of applicant _____

        Participant 15—rating of applicant _____

        Participant 16—rating of applicant _____

Concept and Goal

This activity examines how gender can affect attributions of success for some cognitive tasks. You should complete the activity individually, but the class should analyze the results and review the discussion questions.

Instructions

Attributions are explanations about the causes of behavior. There are four possible attributions for a successful outcome on a task (e.g., a college examination): (1) ability, (2) effort, (3) task easiness, and (4) luck. Read the following passage and answer the questions posed.

Think about the last time you received a good grade on a test. Four possible factors could have been responsible for your success; those factors are listed below. You have 100 points to divide among these four factors. Assign points to reflect the extent to which each factor contributed to your success; the points must add up to 100.

_____ I have high ability for the subject that was covered on that test.

_____ I put a lot of effort into studying for that test.

_____ The test was easy.

_____ It was just luck.

Your instructor will give you instructions to complete the activity.

Discussion Questions

1) What attributions can be supplied for successful task performance?

2) What attributions can be supplied for unsuccessful task performance?

3) Were there gender differences in your class's responses for this activity? If so, explain the nature of the differences.

4) If there were no differences, give possible reasons why. Do you think there would have been gender differences in the class's responses if the class had been told to think of a time when they received a good grade on a specific test (e.g., mathematics, spatial, or verbal test). If so, explain.

References

Matlin, Margaret. 1996. *The psychology of women.* 3rd ed. Fort Worth, TX: Harcourt Brace.

Source: Activity by Matlin, M. 1996. *The psychology of women.* 3rd ed., 205. Fort Worth, TX: Harcourt Brace.

IQ Extremes

Concept and Goal

This activity allows you to critically analyze the research on sex and IQ scores. You should read the passage and then prepare the discussion questions for class interaction.

Instructions

Read the following passage from Shenker, Goss, & Bernstein's *Instructor's Manual* to accompany Bernstein's *Psychology*, 4th edition 1997, and answer the discussion questions.

Males and IQ Extremes

In 1894, Ellis observed that there appeared to be a greater number of eminent men than there were eminent women. He concluded that men were, on average, more intelligent than women. Although this argument was heavily criticized as being based on nonscientific measures, more recent studies using controlled data collection methods and modern IQ tests have found that men tend to dominate the higher ranges of IQ test scores. What do such findings mean?

Hedges and Nowell (1995) speculated that male IQ scores may simply be more variable than female IQ scores. To explore this issue, they reviewed six   large-scale IQ studies. These studies had in common that they had used modern survey methods and modern IQ tests, they were conducted over the last 35 years, and they examined representative samples of adolescents and young adults in the United States. Altogether, across all these studies, Hedges and Nowell reviewed IQ scores of over 220,000 people to investigate possible sex differences in IQ scores.

The results showed that there were very small sex differences in IQ scores, with males averaging slightly higher than females for some subjects and females slightly higher than males for other subjects. Despite these rather small and inconsistent sex differences in average IQ scores, there were sizable sex differences in variability of IQ scores—the degree to which scores are spread out away from the average. Male IQ scores varied more dramatically compared to female IQ scores. The data showed that while there are apparently more male than female geniuses, there are also apparently more mentally impaired males than females. Males were as much as eight to ten times more likely than females to occupy the upper 10 percent of IQ scores, and also just as likely to occupy the lower 10 percent of IQ scores. Moreover, these patterns of sex differences in averages and variability appeared to be consistent across the various studies reviewed, suggesting that the pattern has been stable over the past 35 years.

Discussion Questions

1)	Why was Ellis' conclusion that there were more eminent men than women problematic?

2)	What do the data from the Hedges and Nowell study say to you? What conclusions are reasonable from these data?

3)	Can you think of questions raised by the results of the Hedges and Nowell study? List them.

References

Ellis, H. 1984. *Man and woman: A study of human secondary sexual characteristics.* London: Walter Scott.

Hedges, L.V., and Nowell, A. 1995. Sex differences in mental test scores, variability, and numbers of high-scoring individuals. *Science* 269: 41–45.

Shenker, J., Goss, S., and Bernstein, D. 1997. *Instructor's manual* to accompany Bernstein's *Psychology.* 4th ed. Boston, MA: Houghton Mifflin.

Activity
37

Eating Habits

Concept and Goal

This activity demonstrates how the various ethnic and cultural groups in this country have contributed to a diversity of eating habits among Americans. You should answer the items individually, but the class should review and discuss the answers and discussion questions.

Instructions

Food habits are the ways in which humans use food; this includes the food that people choose to eat as well as how food is obtained, stored, prepared, served, and consumed. The U.S. contains many different ethnic and cultural groups, so the foods and food habits of Americans are diverse. "Melting pot" has been used to describe the mix of populations living in the United States. Food and food habits are a part of that mix. Although Americans of every cultural background enjoy hamburgers and fries, American cuisine goes far beyond meat and potatoes. (As suggested by their names, not even hamburgers and french fries are American in origin. Chopped beef steaks were introduced to the United States from Hamburg, Germany in the late 1800s, and the sandwich became popularized at the St. Louis World's Fair). Just as it is impossible to describe the American diet, it can't be said that members of American minority groups eat only their traditional food. We eat many of the foods, beverages, and dishes listed below. Although many have become part of the American diet, they originated in other parts of the world and serve as diet staples there. Identify the country where the following food, beverages, and dishes originated.

_____ 1. fish and chips

_____ 2. egg (spring) roll

_____ 3. nachos

_____ 4. dijon mustard

_____ 5. ravioli

_____ 6. grits

_____ 7. pizza

_____ 8. goulash

_____ 9. tacos

_____ 10. crepes suzette

_____ 11. quiche

_____ 12. soy sauce

_____ 13. shish kebab

_____ 14. teriyaki sauce

_____ 15. shrimp scampi

_____ 16. fried okra

_____ 17. rum

Key
1.   Great Britain
2.   China
3.   Mexico
4.   France
5.   Italy
6.   America (Native Americans)
7.   Italy
8.   Hungary
9.   Mexico
10. France
11. France
12. China
13. Greece/Middle East
14. Japan
15. Italy
16. West Africa
17. Caribbean

Discussion Questions
1)   Why can American eating habits be considered a "melting pot?"

2)   Can you think of American dishes that consist of food combinations from more than one country, e.g., tofu lasagna?

3)   Can you think of American dishes that originated in countries not listed in this activity?

References

Kittler, P. G., and Sucher, K. 1989. *Food and culture in America*. New York: Van Nostrand Reinhold.

Concept and Goal

This activity is designed to familiarize you with similarities and differences among cultures in mate preferences. You should read the passage and then prepare the discussion questions for class interaction.

Instructions

Read the following passage from Buss's article from *Behavioral and Brain Sciences* (1989). Buss collected data from more than 10,000 people in 37 cultures on six continents and five islands. After reading the passage, answer the discussion questions.

Mate Preferences

People were asked to indicate how desirable 31 characteristics were in a potential marriage partner. Two instruments were used. For the first rating instrument, participants indicated how important each of 18 characteristics was on a scale ranging from "0" (irrelevant or unimportant) to "3" (indispensable). The second instrument requested participants to rank each of 13 characteristics as "1" (most desirable) to "3" (least desirable).

When the data from each of the 37 cultures was analyzed, people in nearly every culture agreed about which were the top few most desirable characteristics. Not only was there agreement across cultures on the top few, men and women were identical in nearly all of the 37 cultures on these most valued attributes. Everywhere, both men and women wanted a mate who was kind and understanding, intelligent, had an exciting personality, and was healthy. Universally, both men and women wanted love and attraction, and a mate who possessed emotional stability and maturity, dependability, a pleasing disposition, and good health. (Love was just as highly prized by the Chinese, Indonesians, Zambians, Nigerians, Iranians, Palestinians, etc.) At least with respect to these characteristics, people everywhere have roughly the same desires.

Not all characteristics showed uniformity across cultures. Indeed, for a few characteristics, what people desired in potential mates varied tremendously across cultures. Chastity—the lack of previous sexual intercourse—proved to be the characteristic most variable across cultures.

Chastity: No Previous Sexual Intercourse
(0 = Irrelevant/Unimportant, 3= Indispensable)

China	Men 2.5	Women 2.5
Palestinian/Arabs	Men 2.3	Women 1.0
Zambia	Men 1.5	Women 1.0
Spain	Men 0.7	Women 0.4
Italy	Men 0.6	Women 0.3
Netherlands	Men 0.2	Women 0.2

Buss expected that men worldwide would value chastity, and would value it more than women. This is because of the differences between men and women in the certainty of their parenthood. Women are 100% certain that they are the mothers of their children. But men can never be entirely sure that they are the fathers. Over thousands of generations of human evolutionary history, this sex-linked adaptive problem should have imposed selection pressure on men to prefer mates for whom their paternity probability would be increased. Valuing chastity might have been one way that men could be more confident that they were the fathers. However, that was not found.

Men and women from the Netherlands, for example, don't care about chastity at all. Neither is virginity valued much in the Scandinavian countries such as Sweden and Norway. Indeed, some people even wrote on the questionnaires that chastity was undesirable or bad in a prospective mate. In China, however, virginity is indispensable in a mate—marrying a non-virgin is virtually out of the question. People from India, Taiwan, and Iran also placed tremendous value on chastity. In between the Western European countries and the Asian countries were Nigeria, South Africa, Zambia, Japan, Estonia, Poland, and Columbia—they all saw chastity as only moderately desirable in a mate.

Cultures, however, do not seem to be infinitely variable in this regard. We could find no cultures where women valued virginity more than men. In fact, in two thirds of all of our cultures, men desired chastity in marriage partners more than women. Culture does have a large effect on how much chastity is valued. In the majority of cultures, though, so does whether one is a man or women.

Although the value men and women place on chastity in potential mates overwhelmingly showed the greatest cross-cultural variability, several other factors also showed large cultural differences. Examples include good housekeeper (highly valued in Estonia and China, little valued in Western Europe and North America), refinement/neatness (highly valued in Nigeria and Iran, less valued in Great Britain, Ireland, and Australia), and religious (highly valued in Iran, moderately valued in India, little valued in Western Europe and North America). These large cultural differences, important as they undoubtedly are, may mask a great deal of variability across individuals within cultures.

Discussion Questions
1) What do the mating traits that are universal indicate about what is important to all individuals?

2)   Why do you think chastity shows cultural variability as a desirable mate characteristic?

3)   Can you think of a mating trait that might be more important among Americans than other cultures?

4)   What does the author mean by the last statement "large cultural differences . . . may mask a great deal of variability across individuals within cultures"? Give an example.

References
Buss, D. M. 1989. Sex differences in human mate preferences: Evolutionary hypotheses tested in 37 cultures. *Behavioral and Brain Sciences* 12: 1–49.

Concept and Goal

This activity is designed to encourage you to think about the influence of culture on something most of us consider to be somewhat universal—emotional expression. This is a small-group activity. In your group, you should respond to the items. The class should then review and discuss the answers and the discussion questions.

Instructions

The following statements are from two novels. The author of this activity, Klineberg (1938), thought that fiction was a good source of descriptions of emotional expressions. Read each statement and write the emotion that is being expressed or described, selecting from the following: anger, disgust or contempt, fear, joy, sadness, shame, and surprise.

_____ 1. Every one of his hairs stood on end and the pimples came out on the skin all over his body.

_____ 2. She drew one leg up and stood on one foot.

_____ 3. His face was red and he went creeping alone outside the village.

_____ 4. He raised one hand as high as his face and fanned his face with his sleeve.

_____ 5. They stretched out their tongues.

_____ 6. She gnashed her teeth until they were all but ground to dust.

_____ 7. He scratched his ears and cheeks.

_____ 8. Her eyes grew round and opened wide.

_____ 9. A cold sweat broke forth on his whole body, and he trembled without ceasing.

_____ 10. He moved one hand around the front of his beard and touched his head with the fingers

   of the other hand.

_____ 11. She was listless and silent.

_____ 12. She stretched the left arm flatly to the left and the right arm to the right.

_____ 13. His nose wrinkled and the corners of his mouth turned down.

_____ 14. Her smile widened until small wrinkles appeared at the corners of her eyes.

Key
The statements are from Chinese literature, not English literature. Below is a list of the emotions Klineberg associated with each descriptive statement based on Chinese culture. Are these answers similar to yours?

Items 1 and 9 = fear
Items 2 and 5 = surprise
Item 3 = shame
Items 4, 6, and 8 = anger
Items 7, 12, and 14 = joy
Items 10 and 11 = sadness
Item 13 = disgust or contempt

Discussion Questions
1) What does this activity indicate about the innateness of emotional expressions?

2) For what items were Chinese emotional expressions similar to American expressions? For what items were Chinese emotional expressions different from American emotional expressions?

3) Klineberg's study is over fifty years old. Do you think historical changes in a culture can create changes in emotional expressions in that culture over time? If so, what historical changes in American culture have the potential to affect changes in American emotional expressions?

References
Klineberg, O. 1938. Emotional expression in Chinese literature. *Journal of Abnormal and Social Psychology* 33: 517–520.

Matsumoto, D. 1996. The diversity of human feeling. In D. Matsumoto, *Culture and*

Psychology, 243–264. Pacific Grove: Brooks-Cole.

Matsumoto, D., and Ekman, P. 1989. American-Japanese cultural differences in intensity ratings of facial expression of emotion. *Motivation and Emotion* 13: 143–157.

Russell, J. A. 1991. Culture and the categorization of emotions. *Psychological Bulletin* 110: 426–450.

Somerville, R. (ed.) 1994. *Emotions: Journey through the mind and body.* Alexandria, VA: Time-Life Books.

Source: Klineberg, O. 1938. Emotional expression in Chinese literature. *Journal of Abnormal and Social Psychology* 33: 517–520.

Activity

40 — Affective Communications

Concept and Goal

This activity examines whether there are gender differences in the expression of emotions. You should complete the scale individually, but the class should analyze and discuss the results and the discussion questions.

Instructions

To measure individual and group differences in expressiveness, Kring and colleagues (1994) designed the Emotional Expressivity Scale (EES). Respond to each of the following statements in terms of how true each is to you. Use the following scale.

1 - never true of me
2 - rarely true of me
3 - occasionally true of me
4 - often true of me
5 - generally true of me
6 - always true of me

_____ 1. I think of myself as emotionally expressive.

_____ 2. People think of me as an unemotional person.

_____ 3. I keep my feelings to myself.

_____ 4. I am often considered indifferent by others.

_____ 5. People can read my emotions.

_____ 6. I display my emotions to other people.

_____ 7. I don't like to let other people see how I'm feeling.

_____ 8. I am able to cry in front of other people.

_____ 9. Even if I am feeling very emotional, I don't let others see my feelings.

_____ 10. Other people aren't easily able to observe what I'm feeling.

_____ 11. I am not very emotionally expressive.

_____ 12. Even when I'm experiencing strong feelings, I don't express them outwardly.

_____ 13. I can't hide the way I'm feeling.

_____ 14. Other people believe me to be very emotional.

_____ 15. I don't express my emotions to other people.

_____ 16. The way I feel is different from how others think I feel.

_____ 17. I hold my feelings in.

Your instructor will give you instructions to complete the assignment.

Discussion Questions

1) Were your results on the EES consistent with your assessment of your emotional expressiveness? If there was a discrepancy between the two assessments, explain why it occurred.

2) Research indicates that females are more emotionally expressive. Was there a gender difference in scores on the EES for your class? If so, why do you think that occurred? If there was no difference, give possible reasons why.

3) Are there benefits to being emotionally expressive? If so, what are they? Are there disadvantages to being emotionally expressive? If so, what are they?

References

Coats, E., and Feldman, R. 1996. Gender differences in non-verbal correlates of social status. *Personality and Social Psychology Bulletin* 22: 1014–1022.

Kring, A., Smith, D., and Neale, J. 1994. Individual differences in dispositional expressiveness: Development and validation of the emotional expressivity scale. *Journal of Personality and Social Psychology* 66: 934–949.

Rosenthal, R., Hall, J., Archer, D., DiMatteo, M., and Rogers, P. 1979. The PONS test: Measuring sensitivity to nonverbal cues. In S. Weitz (ed.), *Nonverbal Communication.* 2nd ed. New York: Oxford University Press.

Source: Activity by Kring, A., Smith, D., and Neale, J. 1994. Individual differences in dispositional expressiveness: Development and validation of the emotional expressivity scale. *Journal of Personality and Social Psychology* 66: 938. Copyright © 1994 by the American Psychological Association. Reprinted with permission.

Activity

41

Perceiving Aggression

Concept and Goal

This activity examines whether there are gender differences in perceptions of aggression in competitive sport situations. Also, the activity allows you to think about definitions of aggression and whether they have a place in competitive sports. You should complete the eight descriptions individually, but the class should analyze and discuss the results and the discussion questions.

Instructions

Eight descriptions of situations or scenes involving competitive sports are presented. Label the behavior in each situation as acceptable or unacceptable on the basis of your own ethical standards. Do not write your name on the paper.

What is your sex?   Male _____   Female _____

_____ 1. A defensive back on the local football team has been repeatedly criticized by his father for not punishing receivers in his zone. He vows to satisfy his father. In the next game, he delivers as hard a hit as he can to a receiver who is in midair, knocking him unconscious and out of the game. Is the defensive back's behavior acceptable or unacceptable?

_____ 2. A young woman tennis player has been beaten badly in the singles' final. She is also in the doubles final and again facing her singles' opponent, whom she thoroughly dislikes. She gets a weak and high return for her serve at the net, and she smashes it at her opponent with obvious delight. Is this young women's behavior acceptable or unacceptable?

_____ 3. An 8-year-old hockey player has been told by his coach that if he does not play more physically, he will be benched. He is checked hard by an opposing defensive player and retaliates by spearing him with his hockey stick. Though he is penalized by the referee, he is cheered by his coach. Is this boy's behavior acceptable or unacceptable?

_____ 4. Two high school girl's basketball teams meet in the regional finals. The only black player on the court is the star on one team. She is constantly heckled when she has the ball. This includes the organized use of racial slurs by the opposing team's cheering section. Is the behavior of these fans acceptable or unacceptable?

_____ 5. The Dodgers are playing the Giants. In the second inning the Dodgers' pitcher hits the Giants' first baseman, because he says this is his plate. When the Dodgers' pitcher comes to bat the next inning, the Giants' pitcher purposefully hits him on this throwing arm. Is the behavior of the Giants' pitcher acceptable or unacceptable?

_____ 6. The coach of a women's volleyball team knows that the star of the opposing team has a very sore back. She instructs her players to spike every shot they can at the injured opponent in an attempt to aggravate her injury and knock her out of the game. Is the coach's behavior acceptable or unacceptable?

_____ 7. During a horse race, a jockey is determined to win the race. At one of the curves, he instructs his horse to run as close as possible toward the boundary of an opponent's lane. They are so close to the next lane that several of the horses and jockeys slightly behind them collide. Is the jockey's behavior acceptable or unacceptable?

_____ 8. A crowd cheers while a basketball player for their team slam dunks the ball into the basketball hoop with great force. A player for the opposing team who is observing while standing underneath the goal is knocked to the floor and injured. Is the behavior of the basketball player who slam dunks the ball acceptable or unacceptable?

Your instructor will give you further instructions to complete the activity.

Discussion Questions
1) Was there a gender difference in the acceptance of sports aggression for your class? If so, why do you think this occurred? If there was no difference, give possible reasons why.

2) What do you think will happen to women's attitudes about sports aggression as they become increasingly involved in sports?

3) Do you think aggression in military situations is a topic analogous to aggression in sports situations? What similarities and what differences do you see?

References
Matlin, M. 1999. *Psychology.* 3rd ed. Fort Worth, TX: Harcourt Brace.
Myers, D. 1998. *Psychology.* 5th ed. New York: Worth.

Rainey, D. 1986. A gender difference in acceptance of sport aggression: A classroom activity. *Teaching of Psychology* 13: 138–140.

Silva, J. M. 1983. The perceived legitimacy of role violating behavior in sports. *Journal of Sports Psychology* 5: 438–448.

Weiten, W. 1998. *Psychology themes and variations* 4th ed. Pacific Grove, CA: Brooks Cole.

Wood, S., and Wood, E. 1999. *The world of psychology.* 3rd ed. Boston, MA: Allyn & Bacon.

Source: Activity by Rainey, D. 1986. A gender difference in acceptance of sport aggression: A classroom activity. *Teaching of Psychology* 13: 138–140. Reprinted with permission of Lawrence Erlbaum Associates, Inc.

Activity

42   *Biology of the Sexes*

Concept and Goal

This activity demonstrates that men and women are not the same. For example, men are more likely to hiccup than women. More boys than girls sleepwalk. Women have only four-fifths as many red blood cells in each drop of their blood. Women suffer more from throbbing migraine headaches, men from piercing cluster headaches. Despite these physical differences, men and women are equal. That is, both sexes are equally important and make equally valuable contributions to society. This is a small-group activity. In your group, you should answer the questions. The class should then review and discuss the answers and the discussion questions.

Instructions

This activity tests your knowledge about the biology of the sexes. Answer the following questions about men and women. An answer key is provided.

_____ 1. Whose hands are warmer, a man's or a woman's?

_____ 2. Whose forehead is more likely to feel warm, a man's or a woman's?

_____ 3. Whose armpits are smellier, a man's or a womnn's?

_____ 4. Whose nose knows this rose from that rose, a man's or a woman's?

_____ 5. Who is most likely to wake in the night with a stomachache, a man or a woman?

_____ 6. Who is gasping for air in the bedroom, a man or a woman?

_____ 7. Who is that sneezing in the living room, a man or a woman?

_____ 8. Whose heart will still be beating when it's 78 years old, a man's or a woman's?

_____ 9. Who is more likely to use both hemispheres of the brain to process information, a man or a woman?

_____ 10. Who is more likely to have red-green color blindness, a man or a woman?

_____ 11. Who is more likely to become sexually responsive when hormone levels are at their peak level, a man or a woman?

_____ 12. Who is more likely to have several orgasms during intercourse, a man or a woman?

Key

1. Usually a man's because, at room temperature, healthy men have a larger flow of blood to their fingers than do healthy women. When a woman warms up, however, the flow of blood to her hands will exceed a man's because her blood vessels are more expandable. Thus, her body can accept 40 percent more blood during pregnancy with no increase in blood pressure.

2. A woman's but it depends on the time of month. Normal temperature of either sex is 98.6 degrees. However, at ovulation a woman's temperature increases about one degree and remains there for 12 to 14 days until just before menstruation.

3. A woman's. Men perspire most heavily on the upper chest from glands secreting only salts and water. Women sweat most heavily under the arms from glands that secrete fatty substances in addition to salts and water. Bacteria digest the fatty substances and their by-products make this sweat smelly.

4. Probably a woman's. The ability to smell, taste, and hear is influenced by a variety of hormones but especially the adrenal hormones. At almost every point in the cycle, a woman's senses are most acute. Her senses become even sharper as the monthly production of estrogen increases, peaking at ovulation.

5. A man, two to one. A gnawing pain in the middle of the night is a common symptom of a duodenal ulcer, still primarily a male affliction.

6. Probably a man. Men below age 55 are 10 to 15 times more likely to suffer from sleep apnea. After age 55, women catch up.

7. If it's hay fever season, probably a man. The people most likely to be afflicted by airborne allergies are 18- to 24-year-old men, 33 percent of whom suffer when there's house dust or pollen in the air, versus 24 percent of women that age. Men of all ages are more likely to be allergic to plant pollens, women are more likely to be allergic to cats and dogs. No one knows why.

8. Odds are, a woman's. As of 1989, life expectancy was 78.5 years for women, 71.8 years for men.

9. A woman. The functions of the left and right cerebral hemispheres appear to be more integrated and symmetrical in women. In men, the left and right hemispheres are more asymmetrical and more highly specialized for different tasks. Research also suggests that the posterior portion of the corpus callosum (the splenium) is larger in females than males. Because the splenium transfers information between brain hemispheres, this may also contribute to more bilateral representation of information for women.

10. A man. In females, the 23rd pair of chromosomes is made up of two X chromosomes. In males, an X chromosome and a Y chromosome make up the 23rd pair. Recessive characteristics normally require the presence of two identical recessive genes for a trait to be displayed. This pattern holds for recessive characteristics communicated on the 23rd

chromosome pair. Females require the presence of two recessive genes, one on each X chromosome. For males, however, the Y chromosome often does not contain a corresponding gene segment to match on their X chromosome. This means that a male can display certain recessive characteristics as a result of only one recessive gene carried on the X chromosome of his XY pair. As a result, they are more likely than females to display the sex-linked recessive characteristics, such as red-green color blindness, congenital night blindness, hemophilia, and brown tooth enamel.

11. A woman. Females become sexually receptive when production of the female hormone estrogen peaks at ovulation. (In experiments, researchers simulate receptivity by injecting female animals with estrogen.) Male hormone levels are more constant and researchers can't so easily manipulate the sexual behavior of male animals by testosterone treatments.

12. A woman. Women are more likely than men to be multiorgasmic. Men go through a refractory period before they are capable of another orgasm.

Discussion Questions

1) Can you think of other biological differences between men and women that were not listed? Do you know what accounts for these differences?

2) The point of this activity is to indicate that although men and women may differ biologically, they are still equal to each other. Can a similar analogy be made when examining differences between different ethnic or racial groups? If so, explain.

References

Rizgler, C. A. March/April 1988. The annotated Adam and Eve. *Hippocrates,* 78–79.

Source: Activity by Rizgler, C. A. March/April 1988. The annotated Adam and Eve. *Hippocrates,* 78–79. Reprinted with permission of *Hippocrates*.

Concept and Goal

This activity helps you to determine the role that ethnicity plays in your life. In this country, people come from many ethnic backgrounds, such as Hispanic, Native American, African-American, Asian-American, and Anglo-American. Although every person is born into one or several ethnic groups, we differ in how important our ethnic status is to us. You should complete the test. After you have scored your test, prepare answers to the discussion questions for class interaction.

Instructions

Phinney (1992) developed the Multigroup Ethnic Identity Measure. It is a measure of how important a person's ethnicity is, how we feel about our ethnicity, and how much our behavior is affected by ethnicity. Complete this scale by completing your ethnicity and answering the following questions.

What is your ethnic group(s)? _____

Use the numbers given below to indicate how much you agree or disagree with each statement. Write the number that gives the best answer to each question.

    1 - Strongly disagree
    2 - Somewhat disagree
    3 - Somewhat agree
    4 - Strongly agree

_____ 1. I have spent time trying to find out more about my own ethnic group, such as its history, traditions, and customs.

_____ 2. I am active in organizations or social groups that include mostly members of my own ethnic group.

_____ 3. I have a clear sense of my ethnic background and what it means for me.

_____ 4. I like meeting and getting to know people from ethnic groups other than my own.

_____ 5. I think a lot about how my life will be affected by my ethnic group membership.

_____ 6. I am happy that I am a member of the group I belong to.

_____ 7. I sometimes feel that it would be better if different ethnic groups didn't try to mix together.

_____ 8. I am not very clear about the role of my ethnicity in my life.

_____ 9. I often spend time with people from ethnic groups other than my own.

_____ 10. I really have not spent much time trying to learn more about the culture and history of my

   ethnic group.

_____ 11. I have a strong sense of belonging to my own ethnic group.

_____ 12. I understand pretty well what my ethnic group membership means to me.

_____ 13. In order to learn more about my ethnic background, I have often talked to other people

   about my ethnic group.

_____ 14. I have a lot of pride in my ethnic group and its accomplishments.

_____ 15. I don't try to become friends with people from other ethnic groups.

_____ 16. I participate in cultural practices of my own group, such as special food, music, or

   customs.

_____ 17. I am involved in activities with people from other ethnic groups.

_____ 18. I feel a strong attachment towards my own ethnic group.

_____ 19. I enjoy being around people from ethnic groups other than my own.

_____ 20. I feel good about my cultural or ethnic background.

_____ 21. My ethnicity is

   a. Asian, Asian-American, Oriental
   b. Black or African-American
   c. Hispanic or Latino
   d. White, Caucasian, European
   e. American-Indian
   f. Mixed; parents are from two different groups
   g. Other (write in): _____

_____ 22. My father's ethnicity is (use letters from question 21)

_____ 23. My mother's ethnicity is (use letters from question 21)

Scoring
Ethnic identity orientation.

1) Reverse individual scores on items 8 and 10 (change 1 to 4, 2 to 3, 3 to 2, and 4 to 1).
2) Add the numbers in front of items 1, 2, 3, 5, 6, 8, 10, 11, 12, 13, 14, 16, 18, and 20.
3) Divide the sum by 14 to obtain your average.

Subscales of the Ethnic Identity Measure are as follows.

> Affirmation and Belonging (items 6, 11, 14, 18, & 20)
> Ethnic Identity Achievement (items 1, 3, 5, 8, 10, 12, & 13; items 8 and 10 should again be reversed)
> Ethnic Behaviors (items 2 & 16)
> Other group orientation (items 4, 7, 9, 15, 17, and 19; items 7 and 15 should be reversed)

Ethnic self-identification (open-ended response), ethnicity (item 21), and parents' ethnicity (items 22 and 23) are not scored but are used as background information.

Discussion Questions
1) What have your learned about the importance of your ethnicity in your life?

2) How might a person with a strong own-group ethnic identification behave in daily interactions?

3) How might a person with a weak own-group ethnic identification behave in daily interactions?

References
Phinney, J. S. 1992. The multigroup ethnic identity measure: A new scale for use with diverse groups. *Journal of Adolescent Research* 7: 156–176.

Activity 44

Famous Personalities

Concept and Goal

You will obtain information on a famous African-American person in the United States and gain experience applying traditional personality theoretical approaches to the understanding of a minority person's personality. This is an individual student activity. After you have completed your report, you are to present a brief summary of your report to the class. The class should then discuss the discussion questions.

Instructions

Your instructor will have you select a famous African-American person about whom there is ample biographical information. Examples are Oprah Winfrey, Malcolm X, Martin Luther King, Jr., Jessie Jackson, or Colin Powell; however, you may choose any important African-American figure. You are to prepare a two-part paper, in which you complete the biography of the individual (part one), and then use the different theoretical models in personality psychology to explain the individual's personality (part two). The theoretical models used can include the following: (1) psychoanalytic—the theories of Sigmund Freud, Alfred Adler, Carl Jung, Erik Erikson, Karen Horney, Harry Stack Sullivan, or Erich Fromm; (2) trait—the theories of Gordon Allport, Raymond Cattell, or Henry Murray, (3) cognitive—the theories of George Kelly or Albert Ellis, (4) humanistic—the theories of Carl Rogers or Abraham Maslow, (5) behavioral/social learning—the theories of B.F. Skinner, Albert Bandura, or Julian Rotter.

Below is a list of some autobiographies and biographies for the African-Americans listed above.

Oprah Winfrey
1) *Oprah Winfrey: Entertainer* by Lois P. Nicholson
2) *Oprah Winfrey: Media Success Story* by Anne Saidman
3) *Oprah Winfrey: The Real Story* by George Mair

Malcolm X
1) *Alex Haley's the Autobiography of Malcolm X* by Harold Bloom
2) *Autobiography of Malcolm X* by Malcolm X
3) *The Autobiography of Malcolm X* by Malcolm X and Alex Haley
4) *The Death & Life of Malcolm X* by Peter Goldman

Martin Luther King, Jr.
1) *I Have a Dream: The Life & Words of Martin Luther King, Jr.* by James S. Haskins
2) *Let the Trumpet Sound: The Life of Martin Luther King, Jr.* by Stephen B. Oates
3) *The Life & Death of Martin Luther King, Jr.* by James S. Haskins
4) *The Life & Words of Martin Luther King, Jr.* by Ira Peck
5) *Marching to Freedom: The Story of Martin Luther King, Jr.* by Joyce Milton

Jesse Jackson
1) *Jesse Jackson: I am Somebody!* By Charnan Simon
2) *Jesse Jackson: A Black Leader* by Patricia Stone Martin
3) *Jesse Jackson, America's David* by Barbara A. Reynolds

Colin Powell
1) *Colin Powell* by Catherine Reef
2) *Colin Powell* by Diane Patrick-Wexler
3) *Colin Powell* by David Roth, Lori Walburg, & Linda Lee
4) *Colin Powell: A Biography* by James S. Haskins
5) *Colin Powell: A Biography* by Howard Means
6) *Colin Powell: A Man of Quality* by Libby Hughes

Discussion Questions

1) What did you learn about the famous African-Americans that were researched by you and your classmates?

2) What aspects of a minority person's life can be easily explained based on traditional personality theories?

3) Were there aspects of a minority person's life that could not be easily explained based on traditional personality theories? If so, explain.

References

Allen, Bem. 1997. *Personality theories: Development, growth, and diversity.* 2nd ed. Boston: Allyn & Bacon.

45

Who Am I?

Concept and Goal

This activity allows you to examine yourself. Specifically, you are encouraged to determine if your identity is individualistic or collectivistic. The influence of culture on identity is also explored. You should complete the activity and prepare the discussion questions for class interaction.

Instructions

Write 20 different statements in response to the question (addressed to yourself), "Who am I?" Begin each statement with "I am ...." Respond as if you are giving answers to yourself, not to someone else. Write your answers in the order that they occur to you. Do not worry about importance or logic. Go fairly fast.

Scoring

After completing this activity, count the number of answers that are linked to a social entity (for example, "I am a son" or "I am a Roman Catholic") and count the number of answers that are linked to personal characteristics (for example, "I am outgoing" or "I am a person who sets high goals for myself"). Also note how high in your list answers occur. Collectivists define their identity mostly in terms of family and social groups. Individualists give priority to personal goals and define their identity mostly in terms of their personal attributes.

Discussion Questions

1) Based on this activity, would you describe yourself as an individualist or collectivist?

2) Can you think of phrases in the English language that foster individualism? List the phrases.

3) Can you think of phrases in the English language that foster collectivism? List the phrases.

4) Was it easier to think of English phrases reflecting individualism or collectivism? Why?

5)   In general, is American society individualistic or collectivistic?

References

Brislin, R. 1988. Increasing awareness of class, ethnicity, and race by expanding on students' own experience. In I. S. Cohen (ed.), *The G. Stanley Hall Lecture Series* (Vol. 8, 137–180). Washington, DC: American Psychological Association.

Hofstede, G. 1983. Dimensions of national cultures in 50 countries and three regions. In J. Deregowski, S. Dziurawiec, and R. Annis (eds.), *Explications in Cross-Cultural Psychology*. Lisse, Netherlands: Swets & Zietlinger.

Activity

46   *Broadening the Ego Identity Concept*

Concept and Goal

This activity will assist you in broadening Erikson's concept of ego identity vs. role confusion. Erikson assumes that during late adolescence one forms a sense of self. Erikson's concept of ego identity considers factors such as one's vocational aspirations and religious and political ideologies. You will be encouraged to incorporate some lesser-considered factors, such as sexual identity, sexual orientation, ethnic orientation, etc. This is a small-group activity. Your group should prepare the discussion questions for class interaction.

Instructions

After you have read the appropriate sections in your introduction to psychology textbook and/or your instructor has explained Erikson's theory of ego identity versus role confusion, you will be randomly assigned to a group of 5–6 students to think about the process of developing an identity. As a group, answer the following discussion questions. This activity encourages you to think about and discuss issues that may have an impact on the development of ego identity. One person in the group should take notes about the major points that arise in the discussion.

Discussion Questions

1) Is Erikson right about how ego identity develops? What factors are important in developing ego identity?

2) Do women follow the same path in ego identity as men? How might their ego identity development be similar to that of men, and how may it differ?

3) Is there a cohort effect? (Do women in the current generation have an easier or harder time developing a sense of self than women in your parents' generation? What about men)?

4) Think about sexual orientation. Would this be a factor in ego identity development? How might the process for gay individuals be similar to and different from those individuals with a heterosexual orientation?

5) Think of individuals from various ethnic and religious backgrounds. Would issues of developing a sense of personal identity differ among individuals who live in a culture in which they are in the minority?

6) Does an individual who has been adopted follow a different path in ego development? Would it be easier or harder to develop a sense of self than if reared by one's biological parents?

References

Erikson, E. H. 1968. *Identity, youth, and crisis.* New York: Norton.

Kalat, J. 1999. *Introduction to psychology.* 5th ed. Pacific Grove, CA: Brooks Cole.

Marcia, J. E. 1980. Identity in adolescence. In J. Adelson (ed.), *Handbook of Adolescent Psychology,*159–187. New York: Wiley.

Matlin, M. 1999. *Psychology.* 3rd ed. Fort Worth, TX: Harcourt Brace.

Myers, D. 1998. *Psychology.* 5th ed. New York: Worth.

Weiten, W. 1998. *Psychology themes and variations,* 4th ed. Pacific Grove, CA: Brooks Cole.

Wood, S., and Wood, E. 1999. *The world of psychology,* 3rd ed. Boston, MA: Allyn & Bacon.

Source: Activity reprinted with the permission of Janice Kennedy, Ph.D., Georgia Southern University.

Concept and Goal

This activity presents Sigmund Freud's portrayal of the female personality. It also examines critiques and defending positions of Freud's theory on women. You should read the passage and prepare the discussion questions for class interaction.

Instructions

Read the following passage from Jerry Burger's *Personality,* 3rd edition (1993), and answer the discussion questions.

The Freudian View of Women

Karen Horney was a student of psychoanalysis. Psychoanalysis is a type of psychotherapy developed by Sigmund Freud during the late 1800s and early 1900s in Vienna, Austria. Psychoanalysis focuses on uncovering the unconscious material responsible for a patient's disorder. However, Horney was one of the earliest critics of Freud's portrayal of women. While writers still debate the extent to which Freud believed that women were inferior to men, it is clear that he often described females in terms that at least implied their inferiority. At various places in his work, he suggested that women develop weaker superegos (the part of a person's personality that represents one's conscience), that neurosis in women is more difficult to cure, and that women suffer from penis envy (a women's desire to have a penis and be like a man).

Rejection of some of these views came initially from female psychoanalysts such as Horney and Clara Thompson. Thompson argued that Freud saw women only as a counterpart to men. Thus, instead of accepting childbearing as an important function, Freud described it as compensation for the woman's lack of a penis. Thompson, like Horney, also said that Freud confused the role women were relegated to during his era with a woman's true potential.

Later critics have pointed out some of the long-term influence that Freudian views about women may have had. Because Freudian thinking has influenced generations of psychotherapists and permeated 20th century thought, these derogatory images of women could be damaging to women generally. Therapists convinced that female patients are naturally inclined toward submissiveness and are of weaker moral character may attempt to get these patients to accept their lot instead of pursuing masculine interests. According to Thompson, women growing up in an environment in which they were assumed to be inferior by women as well as men may continue to unconsciously accept that inferiority, even after they have consciously freed themselves from that view. Defenders of Freud point out, however, that he may merely have been a spokesperson for the male-dominant attitudes of his day, rather than an active shaper of those attitudes.

Discussion Questions

1) According to the passage, what evidence do critics point to in suggesting that Freud's portrayal of women is negative?

2) According to the passage, what evidence is used by critics to counter Freud's notions that women are inferior?

3) What are your views on Freud's theories? Based on your knowledge of Freud, do you think Freud's theories are chauvinistic?

4) If you were asked to defend Freud's view on women, what would you say?

References

Burger, J. M. 1993. *Personality*, 3rd ed. Pacific Grove, CA: Brooks Cole.

Source: Passage based on Burger, J. M. 1993. *Personality,* 3rd ed., 137. Pacific Grove, CA: Brooks Cole.

Concept and Goal

This activity will help you to explore racial identity development using the Helms model of white racial identity and the Cross and Thomas models of black racial identity. This is an individual student activity. You are to present your oral report to the class, and prepare the discussion questions for class interaction.

Instructions

Your instructor will discuss the nigrescence of black racial identity model (nigrescence is the process of developing a black identity) (Cross, 1978; Parham, 1989) and *A Race is a Nice Thing to Have* (Helm, 1992) white racial identity model. After your instructor has discussed the two models, you will select any movie or book character that illustrates your comprehension of two stages of black or white racial identity (good examples of movie characters are listed in Table 1). You should write a four- or five-page paper that defines two stages of either model and illustrates those stages with statements about the character's actions. On the day that the paper is due, you will give a five- to ten-minute oral illustrated presentation on one of the stages for your movie or book character. (The stages of the Cross and Thomas model of black racial identity and the Helms model of white racial identity are listed below).

Black Racial Identity

1) Preencounter—This person denigrates black culture, idealizes white culture, and denies the personal significance of race or racism.
2) Encounter—This person questions self and others about racial issues. The stage terminates with a decision to restructure one's racial identity.
3) Immersion/Emersion—Phase 1: This person shows extreme anger, idealizes everything black, and denigrates and avoids everything white; this person has an either-or attitude. Phase 2: This person actively defines self according to black and African historical perspectives.
4) Internalization—This person adopts a positive realistic black identity, interacts with others from a humanistic orientation, and fights oppression.

White Racial Identity

1) Contact—This person denies that race is important in society and pretends not to notice another person's race.
2) Disintegration—This person recognizes another person's race but this person sometimes denies it is important or denies its impact.
3) Reintegration—This person addresses racial situations by adherring to the attitude that whites are superior and are entitled to privilege.
4) Pseudo-Independence—This person acts as if she or he has all of the answers for all of the racial problems in society; a person in this stage is quick to deny his/her responsibilities for eliminating racism and is quick to place the responsibilities on minorities.

5) Immersion/Emersion—This person is engaged in an honest assessment of what it means to be white in this society and this person encourages other people to engage in similar self-evaluation.

6) Autonomy—This person has an honest appraisal of race and interacts with all people as human beings. This person also works for the betterment of all people.

TABLE 1		
Movie Characters Exemplifying		
Black and White Racial Identity Stages		
Stage	*Movie*	*Character*
Black Racial Identity		
Preencounter	Imitation of Life	Sara Jane
Encounter	Do the Right Thing	Buggin Out
Encounter	Super Fly	Priest
Immersion/Emersion	Malcolm X	Malcolm X
Internalization	The Ernest Green Story	Ernest Green
White Racial Identity		
Contact	Forrest Gump	Forrest Gump
Disintegration	Guess Who's Coming to Dinner	Matt
Reintegration	Do the Right Thing	Pino
Pseudoindependence	Driving Miss Daisy	Miss Daisy
Immersion/Emersion	To Kill a Mockingbird	Scott
Autonomy	Cadence	Bean

Discussion Questions

1) What are your experiences of your growth through the racial identity stages?

2) How might a person's stage of racial identity development affect their attitudes and interactions in interracial/ethnic situations?

References

Chan, C., and Disch, E. June 1994. *Diversity awareness exercise.* Paper presented at the 7th Annual National Conference on Race & Ethnicity in Higher Education, Atlanta, GA.

Cross, W. 1978. The Thomas and Cross models of psychological nigrescence: A review. *Journal of Black Psychology* 5: 13–31.

Helms, J. 1992. *A race is a nice thing to have.* Topeka, KS: Content Communications.

Parham, T. 1989. Cycles of psychological nigrescence. *The Counseling Psychologist* 17: 187–226.

Richard, H. 1996. Filmed in black and white: Teaching the concept of racial identity development at a predominantly white university. *Teaching of Psychology* 23: 159–161.

Source: Activity by Richard, Harriette W. 1996. Filmed in black and white: Teaching the concept of racial identity development at a predominantly white university. *Teaching of Psychology* 23: 159–161.

Activity

49
Androgynous or Sex-Typed?

Concept and Goal

This activity helps you to determine if you have personality traits that are masculine, feminine, or androgynous. Androgyny is the possession of both feminine and masculine traits. You should complete the test, score it, and prepare the discussion questions for class interaction.

Instructions

Berzins, Welling, and Wetter (1975) have developed a measure of androgyny. Androgyny is the possession of both masculine and feminine personality traits. Some gender role researchers have suggested that people would be happier and healthier if they were less gender-typed and were more androgynous. You can measure your level of androgyny by answering the following questions as true or false.

_____ 1. I like to be with people who assume a protective attitude toward me.

_____ 2. I try to control others rather than permit them to control me.

_____ 3. Surfboard riding would be dangerous for me.

_____ 4. If I have a problem I like to work it out alone.

_____ 5. I seldom go out of my way to do something just to make others happy.

_____ 6. Adventures where I am on my own are a little frightening to me.

_____ 7. I feel confident when directing the activities of others.

_____ 8. I will keep working on a problem after others have given up.

_____ 9. I would not like to be married to a protective person.

_____ 10. I usually try to share my problems with someone who can help me.

_____ 11. I don't care if my clothes are unstylish, as long as I like them.

_____ 12. When I see a new invention, I attempt to find out how it works.

_____ 13. People like to tell me their troubles because they know I will do everything I can to help them.

_____ 14. Sometimes I let people push me around so they can feel important.

_____ 15. I am only very rarely in a position where I feel a need to actively argue for the point of view I hold.

_____ 16. I dislike people who are always asking me for advice.

_____ 17. I seek out positions of authority.

_____ 18. I believe in giving friends lots of help and advice.

_____ 19. I get little satisfaction from serving others.

_____ 20. I make certain that I speak softly when I am in a public place.

_____ 21. I am usually the first to offer a helping hand when it is needed.

_____ 22. When I see someone I know from a distance, I don't go out of my way to say "hello."

_____ 23. I would prefer to care for a child myself rather than hire someone for him or her.

_____ 24. I prefer not being dependent on anyone for assistance.

_____ 25. When I am with someone else, I do most of the decision making.

_____ 26. I don't mind being conspicuous.

_____ 27. I would never pass up something that sounded like fun just because it was a little hazardous.

_____ 28. I get a kick out of seeing someone I dislike acting foolish in front of others.

_____ 29. When someone opposes me on an issue, I usually find myself taking an even stronger stand than I did at first.

_____ 30. When two persons are arguing, I often settle the argument for them.

_____ 31. I will not go out of my way to behave in an approved way.

_____ 32. I am quite independent of the people I know.

_____ 33. If I were in politics, I would probably be seen as one of the forceful leaders of my pact.

_____ 34. I prefer a quiet, secure life to an adventurous one.

_____ 35. I prefer to face my problems myself.

_____ 36. I try to get others to notice the way I dress.

_____ 37. When I see someone who looks confused, I usually ask if I can be of any assistance.

_____ 38. It is unrealistic to me to expect to do my best all of the time.

_____ 39. The good opinion of one's friends is one of the chief rewards for living a good life.

_____ 40. If I get tired while playing a game, I generally stop playing.

_____ 41. When I see a baby, I often ask to hold him or her.

_____ 42. I am quite good at keeping others in line.

_____ 43. I like to be with people who are less dependent than I.

_____ 44. I don't want to be away from my family and friends.

_____ 45. Once in a while I enjoy acting as if I were tipsy.

_____ 46. I feel incapable of handling many situations.

_____ 47. I delight in feeling unattached.

_____ 48. I would make a poor judge because I dislike telling others what to do.

_____ 49. Seeing an old or helpless person makes me feel that I would like to take care of him or her.

_____ 50. I usually make decisions without consulting others.

_____ 51. It doesn't affect me one way or another to see a child being spanked.

_____ 52. My goal is to do at least a little bit more than anyone else has done before.

_____ 53. To love and be loved is of greatest importance to me.

_____ 54. I avoid some hobbies and sports because of their dangerous nature.

_____ 55. One of the things which spurs me on to do my best is the realization that I will be praised for my work.

_____ 56. People's tears tend to irritate me more than to arouse my sympathy.

Key
Masculinity
2-T 3-F 4-T 6-F 7-T 8-T 10-F 11-T 12-T 15-F 17-T 25-T 26-T 27-T 29-T 30-T 31-T 33-T 34-T 35-F 38-F 40-F 42-T 46-F 47-T 48-F 50-T 52-T 54-F

Femininity
1-T 5-F 9-F 13-T 14-T 16-F 18-T 19-F 20-T 21-T 22-F 23-T 24-F 28-F 32-F 36-T 37-T 39-T 41-T 43-T 44-T 45-T 49-T 51-F 53-T 55-T 56-F

Scoring
1) Total the correct responses and divide by the total possible number of correct responses (n = 27) for the femininity scale (feminine proportion score).
2) Then total the correct responses and divide by the total possible number of correct responses (n = 29) for the masculinity scale (masculine proportion score).

Scale
1) High proportions on both masculinity and femininity reflect androgyny
2) Low proportions on both masculinity and femininity reflect undifferentiated
3) A high proportion on masculinity and a low proportion on femininity reflect masculinity
4) A high proportion on femininity and a low proportion on masculinity reflect femininity

For a large sample of male and female college students at the University of Kentucky, the mean "masculinity" score was approximately 17 for males and 13 for females (prior to calculating proportions). The mean "femininity" score was about 14 for males and 18 for females (prior to calculating proportions).

Discussion Questions
1) Does your score on the androgyny scale differ from your ideas of your sex-role characteristics? If so, describe and explain the discrepancy.

2) What are the benefits of being androgynous?

3)   What are the benefits of being sex-typed (feminine and masculine)?

References
Bem, S. L. 1974. The measurement of psychological androgyny. *Journal of Consulting and Clinical Psychology* 41: 155–162.

Berzins, J., Welling, M., and Wetter, R. 1975. *The PRF Andro scale user's manual.* Unpublished manuscript, University of Kentucky.

Berzins, J., Welling, M. A., and Wetter, R. E. 1978. A new measure of psychological androgyny based on the Personality Research Form. *Journal of Consulting and Clinical Psychology* 46: 126–138.

Source: Activity reprinted with the permission of Juris Berzins, Ph.D., Clinical Psychologist.

Activity

50 — *Attitudes Toward Abortion*

Concept and Goal

This activity allows you to examine your attitudes about abortion; it also presents data from various countries on their views on abortion. You should complete both exercises and then prepare the discussion questions for class interaction.

Instructions

This activity is divided into two parts: (1) the Abortion Attitude Scale, and (2) a passage including international data on views toward abortion. Measure your attitudes toward abortion by answering the following statements about induced abortions. In the space beside each statement, place the letter that represents your feelings. An answer key is provided. Then read the passage from Carroll and Wolpe's (1996) *Sexuality and Gender* and answer the discussion questions.

Exercise 1—Abortion Attitude Scale

    A - I strongly agree with the statement.
    B - I tend to agree with the statement but have some reservations.
    C - I am undecided about the statement.
    D - I tend to disagree with the statement but have some reservations.
    E - I strongly disagree with the statement.

_____ 1. Abortion penalizes the unborn for the mother's mistake.

_____ 2. Abortion places human life at a very low point on the scale of values.

_____ 3. A woman's desire to have an abortion should be considered sufficient reason to do so.

_____ 4. I approve of the legalization of abortions so that a woman can obtain one with proper attention.

_____ 5. Abortion ought to be prohibited because it is an unnatural act.

_____ 6. Having an abortion is not something that one should be ashamed of.

_____ 7. Abortion is a threat to society.

_____ 8. Abortion is the destruction of one life to serve the convenience of another.

_____ 9. A woman should have no regrets if she eliminates the burden of an unwanted child with an abortion.

_____ 10. The unborn (fetus) should be legally protected against abortion since the fetus cannot protect itself.

_____ 11. Abortion should be an alternative when there is contraceptive failure.

_____ 12. Abortion should be allowed since the unborn is only a potential human being and not an actual human being.

_____ 13. Any person who has an abortion is probably selfish and unconcerned about others.

_____ 14. Abortion should be available as a method of improving community socioeconomic conditions.

_____ 15. Many more people would favor abortion if they knew more about it.

_____ 16. A woman should have an illegitimate child rather than an abortion.

_____ 17. Legalization of abortion laws should be viewed as a positive step.

_____ 18. Abortion should be illegal in the U.S., because the Fourteenth Amendment to the Constitution holds that no state shall "deprive any person of life, liberty or property without due process of law."

_____ 19. The unborn should never be aborted no matter how detrimental the possible effects on the family.

_____ 20. The social evils involved in forcing a pregnant woman to have a child are worse than any evils in destroying the unborn.

_____ 21. Decency forbids having an abortion.

_____ 22. A pregnancy that is not wanted and not planned for should not be considered a pregnancy but merely a condition for which there is a medical cure—abortion.

_____ 23. Abortion is the equivalent of murder.

_____ 24. Easily accessible abortions will probably cause people to become unconcerned and careless with their contraceptive practices.

_____ 25. Abortion ought to be considered a legitimate health measure.

_____ 26. The unborn ought to have the same rights as the potential mother.

_____ 27. Any outlawing of abortion is oppressive to women.

_____ 28. Abortion should be accepted as a method of population control.

_____ 29. Abortion violates the fundamental right to life.

_____ 30. If a woman feels that a child might ruin her life, she should have an abortion.

Scoring

1) To score the activity, use the following point values for items 3, 4, 6, 9, 11, 12, 14, 15, 17, 20, 22, 25, 27, 28, and 30:

    A = 5   B = 4 C = 3   D = 2   E = 1

2) For items, 1, 2, 5, 7, 8, 10, 13, 16, 18, 19, 21, 23, 24, 26, and 29, use the following scale:

    A = 1   B = 2   C = 3   D = 4   E = 5

3) Now sum your points; your score should fall between 30 and 150. A score of 30 represents an unfavorable attitude toward abortion, a score of 90 represents a neutral attitude, and a score of 150 represents a favorable attitude toward the freedom to choose abortion.

Exercise 2

Read this passage after you complete the abortion attitude scale.

Cross-Cultural Data on Abortion

In some countries, abortion is strictly prohibited or allowed only to save the life of a mother. This includes most of the Muslim nations in Asia, two-thirds of Latin America, the majority of African countries, and a few European countries (Podell, 1990). In countries such as India, Japan, and some of the Eastern and Central European states, abortion is legal under certain circumstances. It is legal upon request (with some restrictions) in the United States, Austria, China, Denmark, Italy, the Netherlands, and the former Soviet Republics. However, rules vary with respect to parental consent, waiting periods, and cost. For example, spousal notification requirements exist in Kuwait, Taiwan, and Turkey (Rahman et al., 1998).

In 1992, two years after the reunification of Germany, East Germany allowed abortion on demand, while West Germany prohibited abortion. As of 1994, the abortion debate continues to divide that country.

In England and Wales, the incidence of abortion has been increasing, and researchers suggest that this may be due to a decrease in the age at which people first have sexual intercourse. In China, nearly half of all women were found to have had at least one abortion; 18 percent had had two or more (Li et al., 1990). In Japan, abortion is also heavily relied upon, but it is used more by married, rather than unmarried, women. This may be due to an underreporting of statistics for unmarried women or because of the low rates of premarital sexual activity for both males and females in Japan (Coleman, 1983). In the United States, approximately 70 percent of abortions are performed on unmarried women. However, in India, China, and Japan, more than 90 percent of abortions are performed on married women (Podell, 1990).

In Brazil abortion is illegal, yet studies indicate that Brazilian women have an equal or greater number of abortions than do American women (*The New York Times*, 1991). The majority of these procedures are illegal, and they cause more than 400,000 cases of abortion complications each year. Many police are trying to locate illegal abortion centers and shut them down.

The least restrictive abortion laws may be in Sweden. In 1975, the Abortion Act was enacted, which gave women the right to choose an abortion and receive abortion and counseling free of charge. The most restrictive abortion laws in Europe are in Ireland. Abortion remains a controversial procedure in the United States as well as in the rest of the world.

Countries, by Restrictiveness of Abortion Law (most restrictive to least restrictive) According to Region, January 1, 1997
Rahman and Henshaw (1998)

To save a woman's life

The Americas and the Caribbean
Brazil, Chile, Colombia, Dominican Republic, El Salvador, Guatemala, Haiti, Honduras, Mexico, Nicaragua, Panama, Paraguay, Venezuela

Central Asia, the Middle East, and North Africa
Afghanistan, Egypt, Iran, Lebanon, Libya, Oman, Syria, United Arab Emirates, Yemen

East and South Asia and the Pacific
Bangladesh, Indonesia, Laos, Myanmar, Nepal, Papua New Guinea, Phillippines, Sri Lanka

Europe
Ireland

Sub-Saharan Africa
Angola, Benin, Central African Republic, Chad, Congo, Cote D'Ivoire, Dem. Republic of Congo, Gabon, Guinea-Bissau, Kenya, Lesotho, Madagascar, Mali, Mauritania, Mauritius, Niger, Nigeria, Senegal, Somalia, Sudan, Tanzania, Togo, Uganda

Physical Health

    <u>The Americas and the Caribbean</u>
    Argentina, Bolivia, Costa Rica, Ecuador, Peru, Uruguay

    <u>Central Asia, the Middle East and North Africa</u>
    Kuwait, Morocco, Saudi Arabia

    <u>East and South Asia and the Pacific</u>
    Pakistan, Republic of Korea, Thailand

    <u>Europe</u>
    Poland

    <u>Sub-Saharan Africa</u>
    Burkina Faso, Burundi, Cameroon, Eritrea, Ethiopia, Guinea, Malawi, Mozambique, Rwanda, Zimbabwe

Mental Health

    <u>The Americas and the Caribbean</u>
    Jamaica, Trinidad and Tobago

    <u>Central Asia, the Middle East, and North Africa</u>
    Algeria, Iraq, Israel, Jordan

    <u>East and South Asia and the Pacific</u>
    Australia, Hong Kong, Malaysia, New Zealand

    <u>Europe</u>
    Northern Ireland, Portugal, Spain, Switzerland

    <u>Sub-Saharan Africa</u>
    Botswana, Gambia, Ghana, Liberia, Namibia, Sierra Leone

Socioeconomic Grounds

    <u>East and South Asia and the Pacific</u>
    India, Japan, Taiwan

    <u>Europe</u>
    Finland, Great Britain

    <u>Sub-Saharan Africa</u>
    Zambia

Without Restriction as to Reason

    <u>The Americas and the Caribbean</u>
    Canada, Cuba, United States, Puerto Rico

    <u>Central Asia, the Middle East, and North Africa</u>
    Armenia, Azerbaijan, Georgia, Kazakstan, Kyrgyz Republic, Tajikistan, Tunisia, Turkey, Turkmenistan, Uzbekistan

    <u>East and South Asia and the Pacific</u>
    Cambodia, China, Mongolia, North Korea, Singapore, Vietnam

    <u>Europe</u>
    Albania, Austria, Belarus, Belgium, Bosnia-Herzegovina, Bulgaria, Croatia, Czech Republic, Denmark, Estonia, France, Germany, Greece, Hungary, Italy, Latvia, Lithuania, Macedonia, Moldova, Netherlands, Norway, Romania, Russian Federation, Slovak Republic, Slovenia, Sweden, Ukraine, Yoguslavia

    <u>Sub-Saharan Africa</u>
    South Africa

Discussion Questions

1)   Is your score on the abortion scale what you expected? Explain your answer.

2)   Was your view on abortion affected by examining the data of various countries' views on abortion (based on Rahman et al.'s table)?

3)   How does your position on abortion compare to U.S. laws on abortion (based on Rahman et al.'s table)?

4)   How would you summarize the data of various countries views' on abortion (Rahman et al.'s table)? Are the countries in agreement or not?

References

Carroll, J., and Wolpe, P. R. 1996. *Sexuality and gender in society.* New York: Harper & Collins.

Coleman, S. 1983. *Family planning in Japanese society.* Princeton, NJ: Princeton University Press.

Li, V. C., Wong, G. C., Qui, S., Cao, F., et al. 1990. Characteristics of women having an abortion in China. *Social Science and Medicine* 31: 445–453.

The New York Times. June 18, 1991. W.H.O. says 40 millions will be infected with AIDS virus by 2000, C3.

Podell, J. 1990. *The reference shelf—abortion.* New York: H. W. Wilson.

Rahman, A., Karzive, L., and Henshaw, S. K.1998. A global review of laws on induced abortion, 1985–1997. *International Family Planning Perspectives* 24: 56–63.

Snegroff, S. 1998. Abortion attitude scale and abortion knowledge inventory. In C. Davis, W. Yarber, R. Bauserman, G. Schreer, and S. Davis (eds.), *Handbook of Sexuality-Related Measures*, 10–12. Thousand Oaks, CA: Sage.

Concept and Goal

This activity discusses the sex differences in longevity rates and reasons for the differences. You should read the passage and then prepare the discussion questions for class interaction.

Instructions

Read the following passage from George Bishop's *Health Psychology* (1994) and answer the discussion questions.

Sex Differences in Longevity: The Hazards of Being an American Male

Although the life span for all Americans has steadily increased during this century, the amount of that increase has significantly differed between men and women. In 1900, women enjoyed a two-year longevity advantage over males (48.3 vs. 46.3 years for females and males, respectively). By 1986, this differential had grown to seven years (78.3 to 71.3)(National Center for Health Statistics, 1989). Overall increases in longevity can be attributed to better nutrition, public health, and medical care, but the increased differential between men and women presents a more perplexing problem.

Although some have argued that sex differentials in longevity are linked to genetic causes, both medical and behavioral evidence suggest that psychosocial factors, particularly those related to the male role, are the most likely explanations (Harrison, 1978). According to this view, the requirements of the male role predispose males to behavior patterns that are detrimental to health, such as smoking, drinking, and taking excessive risks.

Medical evidence for this argument comes from examination of sex differentials in death rates for specific diseases. Among the leading causes of death, those with a strong behavioral component show significant differentials between men and women. For example, men die of heart disease nearly twice as often as do women, and they are two and a half times as likely to die of lung cancer, nearly three times as likely to die in auto accidents, nearly four times as likely to commit suicide, and more than twice as likely to die of cirrhosis of the liver. In addition, men, particularly black men, are more likely to die of homicide. White men are nearly three times as likely as white women to die of homicide; black men die of homicide nearly five times as often as black women (National Center for Health Statistics, 1989).

On the behavioral side, Harrison has argued that the behaviors that contribute to these diseases are ones encouraged by the American male role. Traditionally, this role has included several themes, including needs for superiority, independence, self-reliance, and power over others, through violence if necessary. These role requirements make it more likely for males to smoke, drink to excess, drive recklessly or too fast, be competitive, and become involved in aggressive encounters.

All of these behaviors are major risk factors for diseases showing higher death rates for males.

Discussion Questions

1) This article describes the evidence that females outlive males and concludes that the sex differences in longevity are due to genetic or environmental causes. Which cause does the article favor?

2) Based on the argument of the causes of sex differences in longevity in this article, would females in all cultures have an average longevity that is greater than the average for males?

3) Based on this article's argument, how can males increase their average longevity to equal that of females?

References

Bishop, G. 1994. *Health psychology, integrating mind and body.* Needham Heights, MA: Allyn & Bacon.

Harrison, J. 1978. The male role may be dangerous to your health. *Journal of Social Issues* 34: 65–86.

National Center of Health Statistics. 1989. Health, United States, 1988 (DHHS Pub. No. PHS 89–1232). Washington, DC: Public Health Service.

Activity

52

AIDS

Concept and Goal

This activity examines your knowledge of facts related to AIDS; some questions are included that test your knowledge of AIDS myths concerning females and males. You should answer the statements individually, but the class should review and discuss the answers and the discussion questions.

Instructions

Following is a quiz about AIDS. AIDS (acquired immune deficiency syndrome) is a disorder in which the immune system is gradually weakened and eventually disabled by the human immunodeficiency virus (HIV). Read each statement and respond by writing "true" or "false" in the space provided. An answer key is provided.

_____ 1. The AIDS virus cannot be spread through kissing.

_____ 2. A person can get the AIDS virus by sharing kitchens and bathrooms with someone who has

AIDS.

_____ 3. The AIDS virus attacks the body's ability to fight off diseases.

_____ 4. You can get the AIDS virus by someone sneezing, like a cold or the flu.

_____ 5. You can get AIDS by touching a person with AIDS.

_____ 6. A person who got the AIDS virus from shooting up drugs cannot give the virus to someone

by having sex.

_____ 7. Most types of birth control also protect against getting the AIDS virus.

_____ 8. AIDS can be caused by inheriting a bad gene.

_____ 9. Condoms make intercourse completely safe.

_____ 10. Oral sex is safe if partners "do not swallow."

_____ 11. A person must have many different sexual partners to be at risk for AIDS.

_____ 12. A positive result on the AIDS virus antibody test often occurs for people who do not have

the virus.

_____ 13. Only receptive (passive) anal intercourse transmits the AIDS virus.

_____ 14. Donating blood carries no AIDS risk for the donor.

_____ 15. Most people who have the AIDS virus look quite ill.

The remainder of the questions address AIDS and gender.

_____ 16. Men can give the AIDS virus to women.

_____ 17. Women can give the AIDS virus to men.

_____ 18. A pregnant woman can give the AIDS virus to her unborn baby.

_____ 19. Male-to-female transmission of AIDS is more prevalent than female-to-male

transmission.

_____ 20. In the United States, sexual transmission of AIDS occurs primarily among gay and lesbian

females.

Key
1. True
2. False
3. True
4. False
5. False
6. False
7. False
8. False
9. False
10. False
11. False
12. False
13. False
14. True
15. False
16. True
17. True
18. True
19. True
20. False

Interpretation
Count your total number of correct responses.

Total correct
14–20—a good knowledge of AIDS myths
7–13—a fair knowledge of AIDS myths
0–6—a poor knowledge of AIDS myths

Discussion Questions
1)   Was your score on the quiz what you would have expected? Were you satisfied with your score?

2)   What did you learn from this activity?

3)   What information did you learn that might be helpful to a female? What information did you learn that might be helpful to a male?

References
        Kalichman, S. C. 1995. *Understanding AIDS: A guide for mental health professionals.* Washington, DC. American Psychological Association.

Concept and Goal

This activity examines your knowledge of facts pertaining to chronic illnesses among an ethnic minority group—African-Americans. Your knowledge of facts related to this group is tested. You should answer the statements individually, but the class should review and discuss the answers and discussion questions.

Instructions

Following is a quiz about the incidence of chronic illnesses among African-Americans. Read each statement and respond by writing "true" or "false" in the space provided. An answer key is provided.

_____ 1. The African-American elderly population is increasing at a faster rate than the U.S. elderly

population.

_____ 2. Elderly African-Americans are concentrated in the midwest.

_____ 3. A greater percentage of black elderly are institutionalized compared to white Americans.

_____ 4. Aged African-Americans who live alone or with nonrelatives are among the most

economically deprived groups in the U.S.

_____ 5. Heart disease is the leading cause of death among elderly African-Americans.

_____ 6. Blacks have lower incidences and prevalence rates of cancer compared to whites.

_____ 7. The death rate for lung cancer for black males is approximately 50 percent higher

compared to white males.

_____ 8. Stroke is the third leading cause of death in black populations.

_____ 9. The majority of African-Americans who are diagnosed with diabetes are overweight

women.

_____ 10. Half of African-Americans who are aware of their hypertension are in treatment.

_____ 11. African-American elderly persons have virtually no coping strategies to assist them in coping with illnesses during their later years.

Key

1. True. The U.S. elderly population is expected to increase by 14%, or from 30.5 million to 34.9 million, between 1988 to 2000, while the African-American population is expected to increase by 40%, or from 2.5 million to 3.5 million.
2. False. Elderly African-Americans are concentrated in the southeastern states (59%) and the remaining (41%) live in the northcentral and northeastern states.
3. False. Three percent of elderly African-Americans are institutionalized compared to 5% of white American elderly. A variety of reasons for this are suggested by research, including a lack of financial resources and knowledge of services, health beliefs and attitudes, discrimination, and suspicion and distrust of social institutions.
4. True. In 1989, 91% of older African-American females living alone or with nonrelatives were either classified as poor, marginally poor, or economically vulnerable. Among elderly African-American males living alone and with nonrelatives, approximately 78% were either poor, marginally poor or economically vulnerable.
5. True. Heart disease and stroke account for approximately 24% of the deaths among black males and 41% among black females.
6. False. Incidence and prevalence rates are significantly higher in blacks than whites. This difference is more obvious in males. Blacks have the lowest survival rates; these racial differences are explained more by social and environmental factors than genetics. Native Americans have the lowest overall cancer rates among U.S. populations.
7. True. Heavy smoking and the tendency to delay treatment may be contributing factors.
8. True. Research shows that African-Americans between the ages of 35 to 74 are more likely to die from strokes than white Americans. Epidemiological research showed a decline in stroke mortality in blacks before the early 1980s and an increase after the early 1980s.
9. True. Research shows that black females have the highest rate of diabetes. Obesity is the major risk factor for diabetes. Low socioeconomic status and race (being a minority) are positive predictors of obesity.
10. False, only about 20% of those who are aware are in treatment. And of the 20% in treatment, less than 10% have their blood pressure under control. Non-compliance is a serious problem among black elderly individuals. A variety of factors are related to non-compliance. Some patients do not comply with the medical regimen. A variety of factors may contribute to why patients terminate treatment: lack of trust, health beliefs, barriers to receiving medical care, and knowledge of illness.
11. False. African-American elderly persons have a variety of coping strategies that help them cope with chronic illnesses as they get older. They highly value the family as a system of mutual support and aid and they use religion as a source of strength. The use of religion as a way of coping has a long history in African-American culture, with roots in the slave experience. The African-American church came to fulfill needs and functions once met by religion-based tribal and community organizations that African-Americans brought from Africa.

Interpretation

Count your total number of correct responses.

Total correct
8–11—a good knowledge of African-Americans and their chronic illnesses
4–7—a fair knowledge of African-Americans and their chronic illnesses
0–3—a poor knowledge of African-Americans and their chronic illnesses

Discussion Questions
1)   Was your score on the quiz what you would have expected? Were you satisfied with your score?

2)   What did you learn from this activity?

3)   If you were a health care worker working with a poor African-American population, what information would you provide them given what you have learned from this activity?

References
        Belgrave, F., and Lewis, D. 1994. The role of social support in compliance and other health behaviors for African-Americans with chronic illnesses. *Journal of Health and Social Policy* 5: 55–68.
        Richardson, J. 1990. Aging and health: Black American elders. SGEC working paper series #6. *Ethnogeriatric Reviews.* Stanford, CA: Stanford Geriatric Education Group.
        Ruiz, D. S. 1995. Chronic disease epidemiology among elderly black Americans. *The Western Journal of Black Studies* 19: 37–47.

Activity
54
Curanderismo

Concept and Goal

This activity describes the beliefs about illness and healing held by many Mexican-Americans in the Southwestern United States. You should read the passage and prepare the discussion questions for class interaction.

Instructions

Read the following passage from George Bishop's *Health Psychology* (1994) and answer the discussion questions.

Curanderismo: Folk Medicine Among Mexican-Americans

One of the fastest growing ethnic groups in the United States is Mexican-Americans, many of whom live in the Southwest. A significant part of the Mexican-American cultural heritage is the system of folk medicine known as curanderismo (from the Spanish verb curar, to heal) (Trotter & Chavira, 1981). The beliefs of curanderismo have roots in Judeo-Christian religious beliefs, Native American herbal lore, witchcraft, spiritualism, and scientific medicine. Although curanderismo recognizes many of the same diseases as scientific medicine, it sees illness as deriving from both natural and supernatural causes. Thus, certain illnesses, including those recognized by scientific medicine, are seen as the result of natural forces, and are amenable to treatment by physicians or through herbal remedies. Other illnesses, however, are regarded as supernatural in origin. These illnesses cannot be treated by physicians and require the ministrations of a curandero (traditional healer). A curandero is a member of the community who is recognized as having a gift of healing (el don) and who practices traditional methods of diagnosis and healing. This work of a curandero is not limited to physical ministrations but also deals with the person's social, psychological, and spiritual concerns.

Included in curanderismo are illnesses that are believed unknown to scientific medicine and are thus treated by curanderos. Among the best known are ma, de ojo, susto, caida de mollera, and empacho.

Mal de ojo is an illness of children and infants that can occur when someone, especially a woman, looks admiringly at someone else's child. When this happens, the child may begin to show symptoms such as fitful sleep, excessive crying, diarrhea, vomiting, and fever. Treatment of this condition involves having the child lie down and making the sign of the cross over him or her with an egg while the healer recites the Apostle's Creed three times. The egg is then cracked and dropped into a glass of water. The jar is placed on the child's head while the Apostle's Creed is again recited. Finally, the glass is placed under the child's bed. The child is expected to be cured by morning.

Other diseases are believed to be caused by the person's emotional state. For example, susto results from strong feelings of fright. Weakness is the primary symptom of susto, but if the illness lasts for a long time it can lead to the more serious susto pasado, which can include symptoms of stomach trouble, diarrhea, lack of appetite, lethargy, irritability, and loss of weight. Susto can be cured in several ways, including rituals involving branches from a sweet pepper tree.

Caida de mollera (fallen fontanel) is a disease that may be caused by pulling the bottle from a baby's mouth while the child is sucking, by a fall from a crib or bed, or by throwing the baby into the air. In this condition, the area directly under the anterior fontanel (the soft space between the front bones of an infant's skull) is believed to drop. When this happens, the child experiences severe diarrhea and vomiting. Treatment for caida de mollera involves various techniques designed to move the mollera back into its rightful place. For example, the infant might be suspended upside down for one to two minutes so that the mollera can fall back into place. Or a curandero might apply pressure to the child's hard palate with his fingertips.

Empacho is a condition caused by overeating certain foods and is characterized by the presence of a large ball in the stomach. Children under two years of age are believed to be particularly at risk for empacho. When a child gets empacho, he will continue trying to eat but will vomit the food as rapidly as he eats it. Other symptoms include excessive crying, diarrhea, and fever. Treatment for empacho can involve the use of certain herbal medicines and purgatives.

Discussion Questions

1) This passage indicates that curanderismo recognizes that some illnesses are due to natural forces and some illnesses are due to supernatural forces. How does this view differ from the views of the Westernized scientific community?

2) The work of curanderismo is geared to a person's physical, social, psychological, and spiritual needs. How is this view similar to and different from traditional physicians? How is tending to a person's physical, social, psychological, and spiritual needs beneficial?

3) Can you think of other cultural groups who rely on folk medicine or healers to treat some illnesses? If so, list them.

References

Bishop, G. D. 1994. *Health psychology, integrating mind and body.* Needham Heights, MA: Allyn & Bacon.

Trotter, R. T., and Chavira, J. 1981. *Curanderismo: Mexican American folk healing.* Athens, GA: University of Georgia Press.

Zborowski, M. 1952. Cultural components in responses to pain. *Journal of Social Issues* 8: 16–30.

Zola, I. 1966. Culture and symptoms—An analysis of patients presenting complaints. *American Sociological Review* 31: 615–630.

Source: Passage from Bishop, G. 1994. *Health psychology, integrating mind and body*, 186. Needham Heights, MA: Allyn & Bacon.

Concept and Goal

This activity examines whether black American males may be prone to higher levels of stress and thus susceptible to high blood pressure. You should read the passage and then prepare the discussion questions for class interaction.

Instructions

Read the following passage from George Bishop's *Health Psychology* (1994) and answer the following discussion questions.

Blood Pressure in Black Americans: The Role of John Henryism

John Henry, the legendary black steeldriver, is a symbol of the belief that a person can overcome any obstacle through enough hard work. According to the legend, John Henry was a champion steeldriver (a person who uses a steel stake and sledge hammer to make holes for explosives) on the C&O Railroad when he bragged that he could drive more steel than a steam-driven machine being used by a competing contractor. A contest was arranged in which John Henry indeed beat the machine, but afterward died from his efforts (Botkin, 1944). In their work on "John Henryism," James and his colleagues (James, Hartnett, & Kalsbeek, 1983; James, LaCrois, Kleinbaum, & Strogatz, 1984) draw an analogy between John Henry's efforts and those of black Americans who have worked to overcome daunting odds in their struggle for economic self-sufficiency. According to this reasoning, the belief that any obstacle can be overcome by hard work and determination can lead to chronic, excessive arousal when the person is continually required to overcome obstacles such as discrimination based on lack of formal education. In turn, this excessive arousal may be one of the factors leading to hypertension among black Americans, particularly those with limited education.

To test this hypothesis, James and his colleagues (James et al., 1983) developed an eight-item scale for John Henryism, including such items as "Once I make up my mind to do something, I stay with it until the job is completely done" and "I feel I am the kind of man who stands up for what he believes in, regardless of the consequences." This scale was then administered to a group of Southern, working-class black men during an interview in which they answered questions about educational background, life aspirations, and various health issues. In addition, blood pressure measures were obtained. The results showed that men who are high on John Henryism and had fewer than 11 years of education had higher diastolic blood pressure than did those who were either low in John Henryism or had more education.

Another study explored the role of John Henryism in the relationship between occupational stress and blood pressure. The results showed that although black men who perceived themselves as being successful tended to have lower diastolic blood pressure, this was not true for those who were also high in John Henryism. In addition, diastolic blood pressure was particularly high for men who were successful but high in John Henryism and felt that they had been hindered by being black. These data lend support to the hypothesis that hypertension in black American males may, at least partly, be a function of barriers faced by black Americans and beliefs about how those barriers can be overcome.

Discussion Questions

1)   According to this passage, what are some stressors that may lead to hypertension among black American males?

2)   What would you suggest to control hypertension among black American males?

3)   Can you think of other ethnic minority groups that may be prone to hypertension based on stressors in their environment? If so, list them.

References

Bishop, G. 1994. *Health psychology, integrating mind and body.* Needham Heights, MA: Allyn & Bacon.

Botkin, B. A. 1944. *A treasury of American folklore.* New York: Crown Publishers.

James, S. A., Hartnett, S. A., and Kalsbeek, W. D. 1983. John Henryism and blood pressure differences among black men. *Journal of Behavioral Medicine* 6: 259–278.

James, S. A., LaCrois, A. Z., Kleinbaum, D. G., and Strogatz, D. S. 1984. John Henryism and blood pressure differences among black men. II. The role of occupational stressors. *Journal of Behavioral Medicine* 7: 259–275.

Activity

56

"Normal" Sex

Concept and Goal

This activity demonstrates the different attitudes that the sexes have about normal sexuality and discusses the concept "normal" sexual behavior. This is a class activity. You should individually complete the items of the scale, and then analyze and discuss the results and the discussion questions with the class.

Instructions

The following measure assesses your attitudes about "normal" sex. Rate each of the following activities as representing normal sexual behavior in your view by placing either a "yes" or "no" in the blank.

What is your sex? _____ Male _____ Female

_____ 1. Watching X-rated movies several times a week.

_____ 2. Having sex with more than one person at the same time.

_____ 3. Preferring oral sex over intercourse.

_____ 4. Having intercourse with a member of the same sex.

_____ 5. Fantasizing about having sex with a member of the same sex.

_____ 6. Fantasizing about a person other than one's partner during sexual intercourse.

_____ 7. Masturbating in front of a partner.

_____ 8. Having sex somewhere other than a bed (e.g., floor, shower, kitchen, outdoors).

_____ 9. Never engaging in masturbation.

_____ 10. Becoming excited by exposing oneself in public.

_____ 11. Being celibate.

_____ 12. Being unable to achieve orgasm.

_____ 13. Enjoying being physically restrained during sex (e.g., bondage).

_____ 14. Becoming aroused by voyeurism (e.g., Peeping Toms).

_____15. Playing with food (e.g., fruit and whipped cream during sex).

_____16. Dressing in the clothing of the other sex.

_____17. Preferring that one's partner initiates sex.

_____18. Inflicting pain during sex.

_____19. Receiving pain during sex.

_____20. Using sex toys (e.g., a vibrator) during sex.

_____21. Having rape fantasies.

_____22. Masturbating after marriage.

_____23. Not being aroused by a nude member of the other sex.

_____24. Being aroused by receiving an obscene phone call.

_____25. Being aroused by making an obscene phone call.

_____26. Engaging in sex with animals.

_____27. Deriving sexual pleasure from seeing or touching dead bodies.

_____28. Becoming aroused by being urinated on.

_____29. Becoming aroused by soiling the clothing of the other sex.

_____30. Becoming aroused by viewing or touching feces.

Your instructor will give you instructions to complete the assignment.

Discussion Questions
1) Research indicates that we use three criteria in deciding whether a sexual behavior is normal:

a) cultural conventions—what society tells us is appropriate,
b) psychological acceptability—what seems and feels comfortable to us, and
c) moral conventions—what religion or our conscience tells us is appropriate.

What criteria(s) did you use in determining what is "normal" sex behavior?

2) Did the class's results support the idea that males and females differ in their ideas of what constitutes "normal" sex behavior? If so, why do you suppose that was found?

3) If gender differences were not found in the class's data, give possible reasons why.

4) Can you think of other social groups that might differ in what is considered "normal" sex behavior? Explain your answer.

5) Do you think the terms "normal" vs. "abnormal" sex behavior create an evaluation of what is appropriate sex behavior? Explain your answer.

References

Kite, M. 1990. Defining normal sexual behavior: A classroom lecture. *Teaching of Psychology* 17: 118–119.

Strong, B., and DeVault, C. 1997. *Human sexuality.* 2nd ed. Mountain View, CA: Mayfield Publishing Company.

Wilson, S., and Medora, N. 1990. Gender comparisons of college student's attitudes toward sexual behavior. *Journal of Adolescence* 25: 615–629.

Source: Activity by Kite, M. 1990. Defining normal sexual behavior: A classroom lecture. *Teaching of Psychology* 17: 118–119.

Activity

57 *Patterns of Sexual Behavior*

Concept and Goal

This activity examines the cultural differences in the sexual practices of three societies. This is a small-group activity. You should read the passage individually, but your group should prepare the discussion questions for class interaction.

Instructions

Following are descriptions of three societies that vary in their patterns of sexual behavior. Read the descriptions from Hyde and DeLamater (1994) and answer the discussion questions.

Inis Beag

Inis Beag is a small island off the coast of Ireland. It is probably one of the most naïve and sexually repressive societies in the world.

The people of Inis Beag seem to have no knowledge of a number of sexual activities such as French kissing, mouth stimulation of the breast, or hand stimulation of the partner's penis, much less oral sex or homosexuality. Sex education is virtually nonexistent; parents do not seem to be able to bring themselves to discuss such embarrassing matters with their children, and they simply trust that, after marriage, nature will take its course.

Menstruation and menopause are sources of fear for the island women because they have no idea of their physiological significance. It is commonly believed that menopause can produce insanity; in order to ward off this condition, some women have retired from life in their mid-forties, and a few have confined themselves to bed until death years later.

The men believe that intercourse is hard on one's health. They will desist from sex the night before they are to do a job that takes great energy. They do not approach women sexually during menstruation or for months after childbirth; a woman is considered dangerous to the male at these times.

The islanders abhor nudity. Only babies are allowed to bathe while nude. Adults wash only the parts of their bodies that extend beyond their clothing – face, neck, lower arms, hands, lower legs, and feet. The fear of nudity has even cost lives. Sailors who never learned to swim because it involved wearing scanty clothing have drowned when their ships have sunk.

Premarital sex is essentially unknown. In marital sex, foreplay is generally limited to kissing and rough fondling of the buttocks. The husband invariably initiates the activity. The male-on-top is the only position used, and both partners keep their underwear on during the activity. The man has orgasm quickly and falls asleep immediately. Female orgasm either is believed not to exist or is considered deviant.

Mangaia

In distinct contrast to Inis Beag is Mangaia, an island in the South Pacific. For the Mangaians, sex—for pleasure and for procreation—is a principal interest.

The Mangaian boy hears of masturbation when he is about 7, and he may begin to masturbate at age 8 or 9. At around age 13, he undergoes the superincision ritual (in which a slit is made on the top of his penis, along its entire length). The ritual initiates him into manhood; more important, however, the expert who performs the superincision gives him sexual instruction. He shows the boy how to perform oral sex, how to kiss and suck breasts, and how to bring his partner to orgasm several times before he has his own orgasm. Two weeks after the operation, the boy has intercourse with an experienced woman, which removes the scab. She provides him with practice in various acts and positions and trains him to hold back until he can have simultaneous orgasms with his partner.

After this, the Mangaian boy actively seeks out girls, or they seek him out; soon he has coitus every night. The girl, who has received sexual instruction from an older woman, expects demonstration of the boy's virility as proof of his desire for her. What is valued is the ability of the male to continue vigorously the in-and-out action of coitus over long periods of time while the female moves her hips like a washing machine. Nothing is despised more than a dead partner who does not move. A good man is expected to continue his actions for 15 to 30 minutes or more.

The average nice girl will have three or four successive boyfriends between the ages of 13 and 20; the average boy may have 10 or more girlfriends. Mangaian parents encourage their daughters to have sexual experiences with several men. They want her to find a marriage partner who is congenial.

At around age 18, the Mangaians typically have sex most nights of the week, with about three orgasms per night. By about age 48, they have sex two or three times per week, with one orgasm each time.

All women in Mangaia apparently learn to have orgasms. Bringing his partner to orgasm is one of the man's chief sources of sexual pleasure.

Mehinaku

Between Inis Beag, where there is little sex and plenty of anxiety, and Mangaia, where there is plenty of sex and little anxiety, is Mehinaku, where there is plenty of sex and plenty of anxiety.

In the central Brazilian village of Mehinaku, sex is believed to be very fascinating and the culture is highly eroticized. There is an openness with children about sex, and children can easily list the names of their parents' extramarital lovers, who are typically many. The men have a very high libido, leading them to compete with each other for women's sexual favors by bringing small gifts such as fish.

On the other hand, the culture is very gender-segregated. There is a men's house and if a woman enters it and sees what she is forbidden to see, she is taken to the woods and gang raped, in a culture that is otherwise very nonviolent. Women are believed to have a much weaker sex drive than men, and there seems to be no recognition of female orgasm. Women's menstruation is believed to be dangerous.

The dreams and mythic stories told by the people testify to their sexual anxieties—for example, those in myths who engage in extramarital sex typically die in fantastic ways. In reality the people continue with a great deal of sexual activity while feeling intense ambivalence and anxiety about it.

Discussion Questions

1) Based on reading about the sexual practices in the three societies presented, how does the United States compare in its restrictiveness or permissiveness to the people of Inis Beag, Mangaia, and Mehinaku?

2) Although cultures vary tremendously in their sexual practices, there are some sex acts that are condemned in almost every culture. Can you cite several?

3) Why do you think that no society has seen fit to leave sexuality totally unregulated?

References

Gregor, T. 1985. *Anxious pleasures: The sexual lives of an Amazonian people.* Chicago: University of Chicago Press.

Hyde, J., and DeLamater, J. 1994. *Understanding human sexuality,* 6th ed. New York: McGraw Hill.

Marshall, D. 1971. Sexual behavior on Mangaia. In D. S. Marshall and R. C. Suggs (eds.). *Human Sexual Behavior.* New York: Basic Books.

Messenger, J. 1993. Sex and repression in an Irish folk community. In D. N. Suggs and A. W. Miracle (eds.), *Culture and Human Sexuality.* Pacific Grove, CA: Brooks-Cole.

Activity

58

Myths about Rape

Concept and Goal

This activity demonstrates that our desires to believe that we live in a just world often contaminate our attitudes toward rape victims, creating a hostile climate for them. You should answer the items individually, but the class should review and discuss the answers and discussion questions.

Instructions

This measure assesses your knowledge about rape myths. Indicate your degree of agreement or disagreement with each of the following statements in the blank space next to each item. Respond to every statement by using the following scale:

0 - strongly disagree
1 - moderately disagree
2 - slightly disagree
3 - slightly agree
4 - moderately agree
5 - strongly agree

_____ 1. A woman who goes to the home or apartment of a man on their first date implies that she is

willing to have sex.

_____ 2. Any female can get raped.

_____ 3. One reason that women falsely report rapes is that they frequently have a need to call

attention to themselves.

_____ 4. Any healthy woman can successfully resist a rapist if she really wants to.

_____ 5. When women go around braless or wearing short skirts and tight tops, they are just asking

for trouble.

_____ 6. In the majority of rapes, the victim is promiscuous or has a bad reputation.

_____ 7. If a girl engages in necking or petting and she lets things get out of hand, it is her own fault

if her partner forces sex on her.

_____ 8. Women who get raped while hitchhiking get what they deserve.

_____ 9. A woman who is stuck-up and thinks she is too good to talk to guys on the street deserves to be taught a lesson.

_____ 10. Many women have an unconscious wish to be raped, and may then unconsciously set up a situation in which they are likely to be attacked.

_____ 11. If a woman gets drunk at a party and has intercourse with a man she's just met there, she should be considered "fair game" to other males at the party who want to have sex with her too, whether she wants to or not.

_____ 12. Many women who report being raped are lying because they are angry and want to get back at the men they accuse.

_____ 13. Many rapes are invented by women who have discovered they are pregnant and want to protect their own reputation.

Key
All items are false, claims Burt (1980), with the exception of statement 2.

Discussion Questions
1) How do you feel about your responses to the rape myth acceptance test?

2) Burt indicates that many Americans accept the myths in the activity. If this is the case, how would this impact victims of rape?

References

Burt, M. R. 1980. Cultural myths and supports for rape. *Journal of Personality and Social Psychology* 38: 217–230.

Burt, M. R. 1991. Rape myths and acquaintance rape. In A. Parrot and L. Bechhofer (eds.), *Acquaintance Rape: The Hidden Crime.* New York: John Wiley & Sons, Inc.

Activity

59

Sexual Harassment

Concept and Goal

This activity examines if there are gender differences in the perceptions of sexual harassment in work-related situations. This is a class activity. Students will individually have adults rate the scenarios in the handout. The class will analyze and discuss the results and the discussion questions.

Instructions

Two of the popular clichés about sexual harassment are that "men just don't get it" or "women see it, men don't." These clichés describe the disagreement between men and women about what constitutes sexual harassment in work-related settings. This activity presents four scenarios of possible sexual harassment. Give these four scenarios (Handout 1) to a group of adults (approximately half female and half male) and ask them to rate the scenarios for the extent of sexual harassment.

Your instructor will give you instructions to complete the activity.

Discussion Questions

1) Did the results from the class's data indicate that males and females differ in their perceptions of sexual harassment?

2) If gender differences were found, what do these results indicate about the relationships between males and females?

3) If gender differences are found, what do these results indicate about eliminating sexual harassment in our society?

4)   If gender differences were not found in the class's data, give possible reasons why.

5)   Do you think that males and females would differ in their perceptions of sexual harassment in a culture where exploitation and abuse of women is not viewed as wrong or in a culture where views about openly expressing sexual behaviors is acceptable? Explain.

References

Bigg, D. April 30,1993. *Brief for Amicus Curiae American Psychological Association in support of neither party in the case of Teresa Harris v. Forklift Systems, Inc.* Washington, DC: Wilson-Epes Printing.

Pryor, J. B., DeSouza, E. R., Fitness, J., Hutz, C., Kumpf, M., Lubbert, K., Pesonen, O., and Erber, M. W. 1997. Gender differences in the interpretation of social-sexual behavior: A cross-cultural perspective on sexual harassment. *Journal of Cross-Cultural Psychology* 28: 509–534.

Handout 1

Read each of the four scenarios and rate the scenarios on degree of sexual harassment on a scale from 1 (definitely is not) to 7 (definitely is).

1. Professor J. teaches a senior seminar class at a large university. Sandra is a student currently in the seminar. Early one evening, Professor J. encounters Sandra walking across campus. After talking for a short while about a research paper she wrote in his class, Professor J. asks Sandra to join him for dinner during the coming week.

1	2	3	4	5	6	7
Definitely is not						Definitely is

2. John is a manager at a computer company. One of his female employees has taken some personal leave days; her son has been seriously ill. The manager arranges a private meeting with the female employee and they discuss the ill son. After the meeting, the manager approaches the employee and hugs and kisses her.

1	2	3	4	5	6	7
Definitely is not						Definitely is

3. Sally, Bob, Jimmy, Tiffany, and Jeff compose the human resources department of a company; they are all co-workers. Prior to a staff meeting, they are chatting. The conversation focuses on a new female worker in another department. Bob remarks, "she sure is voluptuous."

1	2	3	4	5	6	7
Definitely is not						Definitely is

4. Two co-workers, Amy and Steve, are leaving work. They are outside on their way to the parking lot and it is raining. They are running across the street and Steve touches Amy around the waist as they are crossing the street.

1	2	3	4	5	6	7
Definitely is not						Definitely is

Data Worksheet
Sex _____M _____F
Scenario 1 score _____
Scenario 2 score _____
Scenario 3 score _____
Scenario 4 score _____
For each participant, add the four scenario scores and compute the mean.
Male participants' mean scores _____   Female participants' mean scores _____

60

Homosexual Comfort/Discomfort

Concept and Goal

This activity allows you to examine your attitudes about homosexuals; it also allows you to examine how culture shapes our attitudes about homosexuality. You should complete both exercises and then prepare the discussion questions for class interaction.

Instructions

This activity is divided into two exercises: (1) three scenarios that ask you to examine your feelings about homosexuality, and (2) a passage including international data on attitudes about homosexuality. Measure your attitude about homosexuality by completing the questions following the three scenarios below. Then read the passage from Carroll & Wolpe's (1996) *Sexuality and Gender* and answer the discussion questions.

Exercise 1—Attitudes About Homosexuality

Scenario 1—Homosexuality and Friends

It's Saturday afternoon, you're hanging out, and you hear a knock at your door. You open the door, and on your doorstep is a very close friend. After warm greetings you grab a snack and drinks. The conversation is filled with catching up on what you both have been doing and the latest on mutual friends. The conversation turns serious and your friend of the same gender informs you that she/he is gay.

1. What is your immediate reaction?

2. What questions would you have for your friend?

3. What concerns, if any, would you have about the opinions of other people who may find out that your friend is gay?

4. Would it be easier to deal with this situation if your friend was the opposite gender as opposed to a friend of the same gender? Explain your feelings here.

5. What would you predict will happen (if anything) to your friendship in the future?

6. What other concerns would you have with regard to your friend's future and his/her relationship with family and other friends?

Scenario 2—Homosexuals as Parents

Some people believe that homosexuals should not be allowed to be parents. Children are in their formative years and will most certainly be influenced into a homosexual lifestyle by being exposed to parents who are homosexual. In addition, homosexual parents will most likely have friends who are homosexual. Because the parents and their friends will serve as the major role models for children, they should not be allowed to have children.

Some people believe that there is no evidence that homosexual parents have homosexual children at greater rates than heterosexual children. Homosexual parents can expose their children to heterosexual adults to help their children make decisions on sexual orientation. Finally, most sex research indicates that an individual's sexual orientation is established by age four or five, so homosexual parents can be as effective as heterosexual parents.

1. With which side do you agree?

2. Explain why you agree with a particular side and add to the rationale.

Scenario 3—Homosexuals in the Military

Some people believe that homosexuals (gay men and lesbian women) should not be allowed to serve in the military. Problems with living in close quarters, training for important missions, going to war in combat situations, and esprit de corps have all been suggested by those opposed to homosexuals in the military. The fear of same-sex relationships at the unit level and managing the "fall out" from relationship problems are also concerns of those opposed to gay men and lesbian women serving in the military. Those opposed to homosexuals serving in the military also usually feel this is not a lifestyle to be accepted.

Some people believe homosexuals should be allowed to serve in the military. They contend there is no evidence that homosexuals would have any impact on a military unit functioning effectively. Gay men and lesbian women do not make their sexual orientation an issue in the military just as heterosexual men and women should not make sexual orientation an issue. Heterosexual relationships in the military have the same potential for problems; however, it should not be an issue for either. Moreover, for years gay men and lesbian women (who have been in the closet) have been model military employees with excellent service records.

1. With which side do you agree?

2. Explain why you agree with a particular side and add to the rationale.

Exercise 2

Read this passage after you read and complete the three preceding scenarios on attitudes about homosexuality.

Cross-Cultural Data on Homosexuality

In our society, we tend to place value labels on others based on their sexuality, particularly if it deviates from heterosexuality. We have a natural tendency to believe that others see the world the way we do. Yet, that which we call homosexuality is viewed so differently in other cultures that the word itself does not apply. In many societies, men and/or women have same-gender sexual relations as a normal part of their life cycles. For example in Cairo, Egypt, one can see heterosexual men casually kiss and hold hands. Applying American conceptions of homosexuality and heterosexuality to cultures for whom such ideas are meaningless can be extremely misleading.

Same-sex sexual behavior is found in every culture, and its prevalence remains about the same no matter how permissive or repressive that culture's attitude is toward it (Mihalik, 1988). Broude and Greene (1976) examined 42 societies for which there was good data on attitudes toward homosexuality. Twenty-one percent either accepted or ignored homosexuality; 12 percent mildly disapproved of homosexuality; 14 percent ridiculed or scorned homosexuality but did not punish it; 41 percent strongly disapproved of and punished homosexuality; and 12 percent had no conception of homosexuality at all in the culture.

Discussion Questions

1) How did you respond to the three scenarios examining your attitudes towards homosexuality?

2) Would your responses have been different five years ago? Explain.

3) Was your view on homosexuality affected by reading Carroll & Wolpe's passage presenting cross-cultural data on homosexuality? Explain.

4) Although homophobic attitudes can be a result of prejudice and hatred, can you think of other factors that can lead to a disapproval of homosexuality?

References

Broude, G. J., and Greene, S. J. 1976. Cross-cultural codes on twenty sexual attitudes and practices. *Ethnology* 15: 409–428.

Carroll, J., and Wolpe, P. R. 1996. *Sexuality and gender in society.* New York: Harper Collins.

Mihalik, G. 1988. Sexuality and gender: An evolutionary perspective. *Psychiatric Annals* 18: 40–42.

Valois, R. F., and Kammermann, S. 1997. *Your sexuality: A self assessment.* 3rd ed. New York: McGraw Hill.

Harper Collins.

61

Female Menopause Myths

Concept and Goal

This activity tests your knowledge about menopause or the "change of life" and rids you of any myths you might have about female menopause. The activity also examines the influence of culture on the experience of menopause. You should answer the statements individually, but the class should review and discuss the answers and discussion questions.

Instructions

This quiz assesses your knowledge about menopause myths. Read each statement and respond by writing "true" or "false" in the space provided. An answer key is provided.

_____ 1. The average age for menopause in the United States is between 45 and 55.

_____ 2. Estrogen replacement therapy is recommended for most women after menopause.

_____ 3. The psychological block to sexual activity after a hysterectomy is often a result of "old wives' tales."

_____ 4. When menopause takes place, ovulation and menstruation may not necessarily stop at the same time.

_____ 5. Many women have reservations about hysterectomies because they feel their female sexuality will be negatively affected.

_____ 6. When fibroid tumors of the uterus develop, a hysterectomy is necessary.

_____ 7. Hysterectomy is the only solution for chronic vaginal bleeding.

_____ 8. Hot flashes during menopause or after a hysterectomy are psychologically caused.

_____ 9. A woman in the midst of menopause can expect her sex drive to change dramatically.

_____ 10. If a woman's physician suggests she have a hysterectomy, she should seek a second opinion.

_____ 11. Osteoporosis and heart disease are hereditary—nothing can be done to minimize their effects on the body.

_____ 12. Women who have had their ovaries and/or uterus surgically removed are exempt from menopausal symptoms.

_____ 13. The majority of U.S. women have severe menopausal symptoms.

_____ 14. There is a standard set of menopausal symptoms that are universal to all women experiencing the change of life.

_____ 15. Japanese women report hot flashes much more frequently than Western women.

_____ 16. Japanese women frequently report headaches, shoulder stiffness, ringing in their ears, and dizziness as menopause symptoms.

Key

1. True. Menopause is a natural process of declining ovarian function culminating in the end of menstruation, usually between the ages of 45 and 55 in the United States.

2. False. Current research suggests that menopausal women should carefully weigh the pros and cons of estrogen replacement therapy (ERT). ERT can have many positive benefits in relieving menopause symptoms and providing protection against osteoporosis. However, there is an increase in risk of endometrial cancer with the use of ERT. In addition, women who have uterine cancer or estrogen-dependent breast cancer are not considered candidates for estrogen replacement therapy.

3. True. Many "old wives' tales" or myths surround the entire process of menstruation and menopause. Many of these myths are related to the psychosocial effects of aging in American culture and may cause a disinterest in or psychological block to sexual activity.

4. True. The end of the menstrual cycle does not necessarily signal the end of ovarian release of egg cells. Therefore, many physicians do not consider menopause complete until a woman has gone one or two years without a period.

5. True. Some women feel their sexuality will be negatively affected by a hysterectomy, yet there is no physical reason why this should occur. If a lack of sexual desire or feeling of loss of femininity occurs, it is more likely the result of "old wives' tales," cultural conditioning, or psychological blocks.

6. False. According to the American College of Obstetricians and Gynecologists, a hysterectomy may be performed when the uterus grows beyond the size of a twelve-week pregnancy from a fibroid tumor. A myomectomy is a procedure in which the tumors are removed but the uterus remains intact. This may accomplish the aim of a hysterectomy, yet leave the woman fertile.

7. False. Chronic vaginal bleeding may be treated by a D&C; therefore, this is one option to consider before having a hysterectomy. A "D&C" is performed by opening the cervix (dilation) and scraping the uterine wall (curettage) with a sterile loop-shaped instrument.

8. False. Hot flashes are believed to be caused by decreasing blood estrogen levels. These reduced blood estrogen levels may affect the hypothalamus, causing the blood vessels to dilate. Blood rushes to the expanded vessels close to the skin surface and causes a sudden sensation of heat for possibly a few seconds or minutes.

9. False. Only if she thinks so. Remember, the brain is the most important sex organ.
10. True. Studies have shown that many hysterectomies are done unnecessarily. Therefore, any woman who is informed she should have a hysterectomy should seek a second opinion. There may be an alternate form of therapy.
11. False. Regular exercise and adequate calcium consumption minimize the loss of bone mass causing osteoporosis. Regular exercise and a reduced fat diet may help counteract hereditary tendencies toward heart disease.
12. False. Removal of the ovaries from premenopausal women causes an immediate "surgical menopause" that is often more severe than natural. Removal of the uterus can cause onset of symptoms earlier than if the uterus were intact.
13. False. Only about 10 percent of U.S. women have severe menopausal symptoms of any kind.
14. False. Some symptoms are shared by many women, but women are all individuals and symptoms may vary in nature and degree.
15. False. Only 12.6 percent of Japanese women who are beginning to experience irregular menstruation reported experiencing hot flashes in the previous two weeks compared to 47.4 percent of Canadian women. Fewer than 20 percent of Japanese women had ever had a hot flash, compared to almost 65 percent of Canadian women. In fact, there is no specific Japanese word for a hot flash, and since the Japanese language makes many subtle distinctions about all kinds of body states, this lack of vocabulary supports the low incidence and perceived lack of problem of what most Western women are more likely to report as a symptom of menopause.
16. True. Because these complaints do not appear directly related to the hormonal changes of menopause, it is thought that there is possibly biological interpopulation variations in physical symptoms of menopause and/or different cultures view events differently. It has been found that in Japan the end of menopause seems to have far less significance than it does for Western women.

Interpretation
Count your total number of correct responses.

Total correct: _____
If you had 13 or more correct responses, you have a good knowledge base regarding menopause and hysterectomies.
A score of 9–12 indicates a fair working knowledge of these topics.
A score of 6 or fewer correct responses represents a poor level of knowledge about menopause and hysterectomies.

Discussion Questions
1) What have you learned about female menopause?

2) If you are a female, would you choose to use ERT? If you are a male, would you want your wife to use ERT?

3) Have you learned anything new about hysterectomies? If so, what did you learn?

4) What have you learned about the influence of culture on the female menopause?

References

Papalia, D., and Olds, S. 1995. *Human development.* 6th ed. New York: McGraw-Hill.

Valois, R. F., and Kammermann, S. 1997. *Your sexuality: A self-assessment.* 3rd ed. New York: McGraw Hill.

Activity

62   *Interracial Dating*

Concept and Goal

     As we begin a new century, society continues to become more pluralistic. Nonetheless, interracial dating continues to be controversial. This activity is designed for you to express your opinions on a variety of aspects of interracial dating. You should answer the discussion questions, then pose the discussion questions to a partner or to a friend(s). The class should then discuss the questions.

Instructions

     "Interracial" in this exercise refers to races. The issue of interracial relationships has historically been a difficult one for America. After decades of laws prohibiting such relationships, American attitudes toward them continued to be negative until the present day, when they can be said to be ambivalent at best. Nevertheless, according to available data, such relationships appear to be increasing. This activity is designed for you to reflect on your feelings about interracial dating. Answer the following discussion questions and use the discussion questions to trigger a discussion regarding interracial dating with a partner or a friend or friends of similar or different races. Research indicates that men are more positive than women and the young are more positive than the old (Todd, Mckinney, Harris, Chadderton, & Small, 1992).

Discussion Questions

1)   Do you approve of interracial dating?

_____ Yes

_____ No

_____ Undecided

Explain why.

2)   Do you consider people who date interracially sellouts or traitors to their respective race?

_____ Yes

_____ No

_____ Undecided

Explain why.

3) Do you think mixed-race couples can overcome the problems inherent in such a relationship?

_____ Yes

_____ No

_____ Undecided

Explain why.

4) Have you ever been romantically involved in an interracial relationship?

_____ Yes

_____ No

_____ Currently dating someone of another race

5) If yes, how difficult was the relationship due to outside pressure?

_____ Very difficult

_____ Moderately difficult

_____ Not at all difficult

6) If you have dated interracially, by your perception, who gave you the most difficulty?

_____ Men of your same race

_____ Women of your own race

_____ Men of your partner's race

_____ Women of your partner's race

Other situations (briefly explain).

7) Would you marry someone of another race?

_____ Yes

_____ Currently married to someone of another race

_____ No

_____ Undecided

Explain why.

8) Would you choose to have children with someone of another race?

_____ Yes

_____ Have children with someone of another race

_____ No

_____ Undecided

Explain why.

9) If you are currently dating someone of another race, what attracted you to this person?

10) Do you (now or in the past) date only individuals outside your own race? (Check all that apply.)

_____ Yes

_____ No

_____ A mixture of races

11) Do you think most interracial relationships are doomed to failure? Why or why not?

12) In your opinion, what would it take in a variety of aspects for a long-term interracial relationship to be successful? Explain.

References

Porterfield, E. 1982. Black-American intermarriage in the United States. *Marriage and Family Review* 5: 17–34.

Solsberry, P. 1994. Interracial couples in the United States of America: Implications for mental health counseling. *Journal of Mental Health Counseling* 16: 304–317.

Todd, J., Mckinney, J., Harris, R., Chadderton, R., and Small, L. 1992. Attitudes toward interracial dating: Effects of age, sex, and race. *Journal of Multicultural Counseling and Development* 20: 202–208.

Valois, R. F., and Kammermann, S. 1997. *Your sexuality: A self assessment.* 3rd ed. New York: McGraw Hill.

Source: Activity by Valois, R. F., and Kammermann, S. 1997. *Your sexuality: A self assessment*. 3rd ed., 243–245. New York: McGraw Hill.

Activity

63   *Mental Health*

Concept and Goal

     This activity demonstrates that gender is a variable other than the actual mental health status of an individual that affects judgments of a person's normality and abnormality. You should complete the checklist individually, but the class should analyze and discuss the results and the discussion questions.

Instructions

     Your instructor will give you the instructions for completing the "blanks" in the instruction section. Think of a normal adult _____. Check each item below that describes a mature, healthy, socially competent adult _____.

1. _____ not at all aggressive

2. _____ conceited about appearance

3. _____ very ambitious

4. _____ almost always acts as a leader

5. _____ very independent

6. _____ doesn't hide emotions at all

7. _____ sneaky

8. _____ cries easily

9. _____ very active

10. _____ easily influenced

11. _____ very objective

12. _____ very self-confident

13. _____ has difficulty making decisions

14. _____ dependent

15. _____ likes math and science very much

16. _____ very direct

17. _____ very passive

18. _____ knows the ways of the world

19. _____ very logical

20. _____ not at all competitive

21. _____ feelings easily hurt

22. _____ not at all emotional

23. _____ very strong need for security

24. _____ excitable in a minor crisis

25. _____ very adventurous

26. _____ very submissive

27. _____ not uncomfortable about being aggressive

Your instructor will give you instructions to complete the activity.

Discussion Questions

1) Broverman and colleagues (1970) found that descriptions of males fit the description of a "normal person" and descriptions of females fit the description of an "abnormal person." Does the class's data support the Broverman et al. hypothesis?

2) If the class's data match those of Broverman et al., what are possible implications for diagnosing a person's mental health?

3) Is it possible that the Broverman et al. (1970) data are dated and no longer relevant, given the changes in gender roles that have occurred in the past 30 years?

References

Benjamin, L., and Lowman, K. 1981. Sex role stereotypes and mental health. In L. Benjamin and K. Lowman (eds.), *Activities Handbook for the Teaching of Psychology* (Vol. 1). Washington, DC: American Psychological Association.

Broverman, I., Broverman, D., Clarkson, F., Rosenkrantz, R., and Vogel, S. 1970. Sex role stereotypes and clinical judgments of mental health. *Journal of Consulting and Clinical Psychology* 34: 1–17.

Broverman, I., Vogel, S., Broverman, D., Clarkson, F., and Rosenkrantz, R. 1972. Sex role stereotypes: A current appraisal. *Journal of Social Issues* 28: 59–79.

Clancy, K., and Gove, W. 1975. Sex differences in mental illness: An analysis of response bias in self reports. *American Journal of Sociology* 80: 205–215.

Tavris, C., and Offir, C. 1977. *The longest war: Sex differences in perspective.* New York: Harcourt Brace Jovanovich.

64   *Mental Illness*

Concept and Goal

This activity examines your knowledge of the various demographic factors (e.g., income/socioeconomic status, racial/ethnic group, or gender) that relate to mental illness. You should answer the questions individually, but the class should review and discuss the answers and discussion questions.

Instructions

Following is a quiz on the effect of demographic factors on mental illness. Read each statement and respond by writing "true" or "false" in the space provided. An answer key is provided.

_____ 1. Persons who are of a low income or low socioeconomic status tend to have higher rates of

mental disorders.

_____ 2. Most minority groups tend to have higher rates of admission into state and county mental

hospitals compared with whites.

_____ 3. Minority groups tend to have greater access to private inpatient care in private psychiatric

hospitals.

_____ 4. The median length of stay at state and county mental hospitals is comparable for most

racial/ethnic groups.

_____ 5. Schizophrenia is diagnosed more often among blacks than whites.

_____ 6. Women experience more depressive symptoms in response to economic hardship

compared to men.

_____ 7. Married women with young children are more likely to suffer from depression than single

women with young children.

_____ 8. Social programs, such as welfare and workfare, that intervene to prevent problems, such as

pregnancy and bad parenting, for poor women do a good job of addressing the women's

mental health needs.

_____ 9. Minority women suffer from eating disorders (anorexia and bulimia) at higher rates than

white American women.

Key

1. True. Decades of research have found that poverty is related to psychological distress and the prevalence of mental disorders. Psychopathology is at least two and one half times more prevalent in the lowest social class than in the highest.
2. True. Inspection of 1980 admission rates indicate that whites are admitted to state and county mental hospitals at a rate of 137 per 100,000, blacks are admitted at rates of 364 per 100,000, Native Americans are admitted at rates of 306 per 100,000, and Hispanics are admitted at rates of 146 per 100,000.
3. False. Because of their greater earnings and likelihood of having health insurance, whites have greater access than minority groups (blacks, hispanics, and Native Americans) to private inpatient care.
4. True. At state and county mental hospitals, the median length of stay is 23 days for whites, 22 days for blacks, and 24 days for Hispanics. The median length of stay is comparable across racial/ethnic groups for private psychiatric hospitals and VA medical hospitals as well.
5. True. For all types of inpatient organizations, schizophrenia is diagnosed more frequently among blacks than among whites. The rate of diagnosis of schizophrenia is sometimes almost twice as great among blacks as among whites. Part of this high rate of diagnosis is thought to be due to misdiagnosis by clinicians based on lack of knowledge of the culture of blacks. However, this pattern was almost exactly reversed when examining whites and blacks and rates of affective disorders.
6. False. Although both men and women experience depressive symptoms in response to economic hardship, men experience elevated symptom levels in association with low income levels. It is argued that men's primary role obligation in the family is economic and that success in this role affects well-being over and above its effect on family finances.
7. False. Studies find that women who live in financially strained circumstances and who have responsibility for young children are more likely than other women to experience symptoms of depression. High levels of depression are particularly common among women without confidants, child-rearing assistance, or employment.
8. False. Low-income women are the target of many social programs, e.g., welfare and workfare. Such programs have important effects on factors such as providing information on economic strain, helplessness, role performance, coping strategies, and the functioning of social networks. Yet mental health diagnosis and treatment is rarely assessed or addressed as part of these programs.
9. False. Minority women are far less likely to indicate a fear of being overweight than other women. Overall, the risk of eating disorders such as anorexia and bulimia appears to rise with exposure to Western culture.

Discussion Questions

1) Was your score on the quiz what you would have expected? Were you satisfied with your score?

2)   What did you learn from this activity?

References

Belle, D. 1990. Poverty and women's mental health. *American Psychologist* 45: 385–389.

Snowden, L., and Cheung, F. 1990. Use of inpatient mental health services by members of ethnic minority groups. *American Psychologist* 45: 347–355.

Activity

65   *Schizophrenia, Depression, and Bipolar Illness*

Concept and Goal

This activity allows you to examine similarities and differences in the symptoms and prevalence rates of three major psychological disorders: schizophrenia, depression, and bipolar illness. You should read the passage and then prepare the discussion questions for class interaction.

Instructions

Read the passage from Wayne Weiten's *Psychology Themes and Variations*, 4th edition (1998), and answer the discussion questions.

Are Schizophrenia, Depression, and Bipolar Illness Similar Around the World?

The symptoms associated with schizophrenia, depression, and bipolar illness are largely the same across widely different societies. However, cultural variations are also seen. For example, delusions are a common symptom of schizophrenia in all cultures, but the specific delusions that people report are tied to their cultural heritage (Brislin, 1993). In technologically advanced societies, schizophrenia patients report that thoughts are being inserted into their minds through transmission from electric lines, satellites, or microwave ovens. Victims of schizophrenia in less technological societies experience the same phenomenon, but blame sorcerers or demons. Of the major disorders, symptom patterns are probably most variable for depression. In much of Western culture, depression is experienced as a psychological problem, with symptoms such as despair, sadness, and guilt. On the other hand, in non-Western populations and among ethnic minorities, lower-class, and educationally deprived populations in the West, depression is experienced more often as a physical problem with symptoms such as stomach pain, sleep difficulty, and weakness (Marsella, 1980). These differences presumably occur because people learn to express symptoms of psychological disorders in ways that are acceptable in their culture.

The prevalence estimates for schizophrenia and bipolar disorder, which both hover around 1 percent, appear to be roughly comparable across diverse cultures (Butcher et al., 1993). This cross-cultural similarity may be attributable to the strong biological component in these disorders or to the fact that they are severe disturbances that are more readily distinguished from normal behavior than milder disorders are. The prevalence rates for most other diagnostic categories vary considerably across cultures (Escobar, 1993). This variability is probably due to several factors. First, there are methodological problems in obtaining samples from different cultures that can be compared. Second, even for a universally recognized disorder, such as depression, different societies will use different cutoffs in drawing the line between normality and abnormality. Third, the environmental factors at work in specific cultures, the predominant attitudes, values, family dynamics, and sources of stress, probably foster some disorders more readily than others.

Discussion Questions

1) According to this passage, why are the symptoms and prevalence rates of schizophrenia, depression, and bipolar illness fairly similar?

2) Why do you think symptoms of depression among people in Western societies are more psychological than physical?

3) How does this passage about the similarities and differences in psychological disorders around the world relate to the nature (all behaviors are innate and inborn) and nurture (all behaviors are shaped by environmental experiences) debate in psychology? Explain the passage based on the nature-nurture debate.

References

Brislin, R. 1993. *Understanding culture's influence on behavior.* Fort Worth, TX: Harcourt Brace.

Butcher, J. N., Narikiyo, T., and Vitousek, K. B. 1993. Understanding abnormal behavior in cultural context. In P. B. Sutker and H. E. Adams (eds.), *Comprehensive Handbook of Psychopathology.* New York: Plenum Press.

Escobar, J. I. 1993. Psychiatric epidemiology. In A. C. Gaw (ed.), *Culture, Ethnicity, and Mental Illness.* Washington, DC: American Psychiatric Press.

Marcella, A. J. 1980. Depressive experience and disorders across cultures. In H. C. Triandis and J. G. Draguns (eds.), *Handbook of Cross-Cultural Psychology.* Vol. 6., 237–290. Needham Heights, MA: Allyn and Bacon.

Weiten, W. 1998. *Psychology themes and variations.* 4th ed. Pacific Grove, CA: Brooks Cole.

Source: Passage based on Weiten, W. 1998. *Psychology themes and variations.* 4th ed., 594–595. Pacific Grove, CA: Brooks Cole.

Activity

66

Eating Disorders

Concept and Goal

This activity examines gender gaps in the prevalence and causes of eating disorders in the United States. You should read the passage and then prepare the discussion questions for class interaction.

Instructions

Read the following passage from Ronald Comer's *Abnormal Psychology* (1995) and answer the discussion questions.

The Gender Gap in Eating Disorders

Only 5%–10% of all cases of eating disorders occur in males. Although the reasons for this striking gender difference are not entirely clear, several explanations have been proposed. One is that men and women are subjected to different sociocultural pressures. For example, a survey of college men by Kearney-Cooke & Steich-Asch (1990) found that the majority selected "muscular, strong, and broad shoulders" to describe the ideal male body, and "thin, slim, slightly underweight" to describe the ideal female body. Rodin (1992) found that 41% of females report dissatisfaction with the appearance of their bodies compared to 32% of males. Of course, although the emphasis on a muscular, strong, athletic body as the ideal male body may decrease the likelihood of eating disorders in men, it may create other problems such as steroid abuse or excessive weight-lifting to increase muscular size and strength (Mickalide, 1990).

A second reason for the different rates of eating disorders among men and women may be the different methods of weight loss used by the two groups. According to some clinical observations, men may be more likely to use exercise to lose weight, while women diet more often (Mickalide, 1990). Dieting is the precipitant to most cases of eating disorders.

Finally, eating disorders among men may be underdiagnosed. Some men do not want to admit that they have a traditionally "female problem" and may try to hide their disorder. In addition, clinicians may be less able to identify eating disorders in men because of different clinical manifestations. For example, amenorrhea, a symptom of anorexia nervosa in females, is not an available indicator among men with this disorder. It is much more difficult to test for male reproductive problems, such as low levels of testosterone (Andersen, 1990). How do men who do develop eating disorders compare to women with these problems? Some of them apparently grapple with similar issues. A number, for example, report that they aspire to a "lean, toned, thin" shape similar to the ideal female body, rather than a strong, muscular shape with broad shoulders typical of the male ideal body (Kearney-Cooke & Steich-Asch, 1990).

In some cases, however, the precipitants of eating disorders are apparently different for men and women. For example, there are some indications that men with these disorders usually are overweight when they first start trying to lose weight

(Andersen, 1990). In contrast, women with eating disorders usually feel overweight when they begin dieting, but may not actually be overweight according to objective measures (Edwin & Andersen, 1990).

One group of men who suffer from particularly high rates of eating disturbances are athletes. Their problems are precipitated not by a cultural requirement to be thin but rather by the requirements and pressures of certain sports (Thompson & Sherman, 1993). The highest rates of eating disturbances have been found among jockeys, wrestlers, distance runners, body builders, and swimmers. Jockeys commonly spend up to four hours before a race in a sauna, shedding up to seven pounds of weight at a time. Similarly, male wrestlers in high school and college commonly restrict their food intake for up to three days before a match in order to "make weight," often losing between 2%–12% of their body weight. One method that is particularly common in this group is practicing or running in several layers of warm or rubber clothing in order to lose up to five pounds of water weight shortly before weighing in for a match (Thompson & Sherman, 1993).

Whereas most women with eating disorders are obsessed with thinness at all times, wrestlers and jockeys are usually preoccupied with weight reduction only during the season, and indeed most wrestlers return to their normal weight once the season is over. After "making weight," many wrestlers go on eating and drinking binges in order to gain strength and hydrate themselves for the upcoming match, only to return to a weight-loss strategy after the match to get prepared for the next weigh-in. This eating cycle of weight loss and regain each season has an adverse effect on the body, altering its metabolic activity and hindering future efforts at weight control (Steen, Oppliger, & Brownell, 1988). In addition, the weight reduction of male athletes has been found to have an adverse effect on their nutrient intake, nutrient absorption, renal function, thermal regulation, testosterone levels, and strength (Mickalide, 1990). Another difference that has been found between male athletes with eating problems and women with eating disorders is that male athletes tend to make accurate estimates of their body size (Enns, Drewnowski, & Grinker, 1987). Recent research further suggests that female athletes with eating disorders display many of the same characteristics as male athletes with these disorders (Prussin & Harvey, 1991).

As the number of males with eating disturbances increases, researchers are becoming more interested in understanding both the similarities and differences between men and women (Andersen, 1992). All eating disturbances are capable of producing physical and psychological damage. Thus, they must all be well-researched and addressed in future investigations and clinical work.

Discussion Questions
1) The passage describes similarities between males and females who have eating disturbances. What are the similarities?

2)   The passage describes differences between males and females who have eating disturbances. What are the differences?

3)   The likelihood of developing an eating disorder varies by sex. What other demographic and social variables might affect the likelihood of developing an eating disorder? Explain how each variable you listed might be related to developing an eating disorder.

References

Andersen, A. E. 1990. Diagnosis and treatment of males with eating disorders. In A. E. Andersen (ed.), *Males with Eating Disorders.* New York: Brunner/Mazel.

Andersen, A. E. 1992. Eating disorders in males: Critical questions. In R. Lemberg (ed.), *Controlling Eating Disorders with Facts, Advice, and Resources.* Phoenix, AZ: The Oryx Press.

Comer, R. 1995. *Abnormal psychology.* 2nd ed. New York: W. H. Freeman & Company.

Edwin, D. H., and Andersen, A. E. 1990. Psychometric testing of 76 males with eating disorders. In A. E. Andersen (ed.), *Males with Eating Disorders.* New York: Brunner/Mazel.

Enns, M. P., Drewnowski, A., and Grinker, J. A. 1987. Body composition, body size estimation, and attitudes towards eating in male college athletes. *Psychosomatic Medicine* 49: 56–64.

Kearney-Cooke, P. and Steichen-Asch, P. 1990. Men, body image, and eating disorders. In A. E. Andersen (ed.), *Males with Eating Disorders.* New York: Brunner/Mazel.

Mickalide, A. D. 1990. Sociocultural factors influencing weight among males. In A. E. Andersen (ed.), *Males with Eating Disorders.* New York: Brunner/Mazel.

Prussin, R. A., and Harvey, P. D. 1991. Depression, dietary restraint, and binge eating in female runners. *Addictive Behaviors* 16: 295–301.

Rodin, J. 1992. Sick of worrying about the way you look? Read this. *Psychology Today* 25: 56–60.

Steen, S. N., Oppliger, R. A., and Brownell, K. D. 1988. Metabolic effects of repeated weight loss and regain in adolescent wrestlers. *Journal of the American Medical Association* 260: 47–50.

Thompson, R. A., and Sherman, R. T. 1993. *Helping athletes with eating disorders.* Champaign, IL: Human Kinetics Publishers.

Source: Passage from Comer, R. 1995. *Abnormal Psychology.* 2nd ed., 412 and 424–425. New York: W.H. Freeman & Company.

Activity

67 *Attitudes Toward Seeking Professional Help*

Concept and Goal

This activity examines whether males and females differ in their attitudes toward seeking professional help. This is a class activity. Students will individually have adults complete the questionnaire in the handout. The class will analyze and discuss the results and the discussion questions.

Instructions

Research indicates that people vary considerably in their willingness to seek psychotherapy. It has been said that many people who need therapy don't receive it. The questionnaire (Handout 1) assesses a person's attitudes towards seeking professional help. Administer the questionnaire to a group of adults; include approximately half males and half females.

Your instructor will give you instructions to complete the activity.

Discussion Questions

1) Did the class's results support the idea that males are less likely to seek professional help compared to females? If so, why do you suppose that was found?

2) If gender differences were not found in the class's data, give possible reasons why.

3) Can you think of other groups who are likely to differ in their attitudes toward seeking professional help? Explain the nature of the group differences.

4) What are the implications of research suggesting that males are less likely to seek therapy for their mental well-being?

References

Fischer, E., and Farina, A. 1995. Attitudes toward seeking professional psychological help: A shortened form and considerations for research. *Journal of College Student Development* 36: 368–373.

Fischer E., and Turner, J. 1970. Attitudes toward seeking professional help: Development and research utility of an attitude scale. *Journal of Consulting and Clinical Psychology* 35: 82–83.

Olfson, M., and Pincus, H. A. 1996. Outpatient mental health care in nonhospital settings: Distribution of patients across provider groups. *American Journal of Psychiatry* 153: 1353–1356.

Weiten, W. 1998. *Psychology themes & variations*. 4th ed. Pacific Grove, CA: Brooks Cole.

Source: Questionnaire by Fischer, E. and Farina, A. 1995. Attitudes toward seeking psychological professional help: A shortened form and considerations for research. *Journal of College Student Development* 36: 368–373. Reprinted with permission of the American College Personnel Association (ACPA).

Handout 1

Read each statement carefully and indicate your degree of agreement using the scale below. In responding, please be completely candid.

Your Sex: _____ Male _____ Female

    0 - Disagree
    1 - Partly disagree
    2 - Partly agree
    3 - Agree

_____ 1. If I believed I was having a mental breakdown, my first inclination would be to get professional attention.

_____ 2. The idea of talking about problems with a psychologist strikes me as a poor way to get rid of emotional conflicts.

_____ 3. If I were experiencing a serious emotional crisis at this point in my life, I would be confident that I could find relief in psychotherapy.

_____ 4. There is something admirable in the attitude of a person who is willing to cope with his or her conflicts and fears without resorting to professional help.

_____ 5. I would want to get psychological help if I were worried or upset for a long period of time.

_____ 6. I might want to have psychological counseling in the future.

_____ 7. A person with an emotional problem is not likely to solve it alone; he or she is likely to solve it with professional help.

_____ 8. Considering the time and expense involved in psychotherapy, it would have doubtful value for a person like me.

_____ 9. A person should work out his or her own problems; getting psychological counseling would be a last resort.

_____ 10. Personal and emotional troubles, like many things, tend to work out by themselves.

Data Worksheet

Scores:	Scores:
Male Participant #1 _____	Female Participant #1 _____
Male Participant #2 _____	Female Participant #2 _____
Male Participant #3 _____	Female Participant #3 _____
Male Participant #4 _____	Female Participant #4 _____
Male Participant #5 _____	Female Participant #5 _____

Activity

68

Culture-Bound Syndromes

Concept and Goal

This activity demonstrates the cultural differences in the presence of certain psychological disorders. This is a small-group activity. You should read the passage individually, but your group should prepare the discussion questions for class interaction.

Instructions

Most investigators agree that the principal categories of serious psychological disturbance, schizophrenia, depression, and bipolar illness, are identifiable in all cultures. Most behaviors that are regarded as clearly abnormal in Western cultures, such as the United States, are also viewed as abnormal in other cultures. People who have delusions, hallucinations, are disoriented, and incoherent are thought to be disturbed in all societies, although there are cultural differences in exactly what is considered delusional or hallucinatory. However, researchers have discovered a small number of culture-bound disorders that further illustrate the diversity of abnormal behavior around the world. Culture-bound syndromes are abnormal syndromes found only in a few cultural groups. Some culture-bound syndromes are presented below. After reading about these syndromes, answer the discussion questions.

Examples of Culture-Bound Syndromes

1. Anorexia nervosa—A disorder found in affluent Western cultures that involves an intense fear of becoming fat, a loss of appetite, and a refusal to eat adequately.
2. Type A behavior pattern—A personality characteristic found in Western industralized cultures; a person with this trait has a personality type that includes a strong competitive orientation, impatience, time urgency, anger, and hostility.
3. Koro—A disorder among Chinese, Malayan, and other Asian males that involves an obsessive fear that one's penis will withdraw into one's abdomen.
4. Windigo—A disorder among Algonquin Native American cultures that involves an intense craving for human flesh and fear that one will turn into a cannibal.
5. Wind illness—A disorder among Chinese populations that is characterized by an morbid fear of the cold, especially the wind.
6. Ghost sickness—A disorder among Navajo Native Americans in which loss of consciousness occurs that is believed to be caused by witches and malevolent supernatural powers.
7. Falling out—A blackout disorder that occurs as a result of coping with life's traumatic events; this disorder is present among certain ethnic populations in the United States (Southern African-Americans and Afro-Caribbeans).
8. Ori Ode—A disorder among Nigerians in which they report sensations of an organism crawling in the brain, palpitations, and noises in the ears believed to be caused by evil spirits.
9. Taijin kyofusho—a Japanese syndrome characterized by intense fear that one's appearance, body odor, facial expressions, or bodily movements may be offensive to someone. This leads to social withdrawal and avoidance.

Discussion Questions

1) Some scientists argue that psychological disorders are much the same around the world and that basic standards of normality and abnormality are universal across cultures. Other scientists argue that criteria of mental illness vary greatly across cultures and that there are no universal standards of normality and abnormality. What do the culture-bound syndromes suggest about this argument?

2) Can you think of any psychological disorders other than those mentioned (anorexia and type A behavior) that might be seen only in our culture? If so, name and describe them.

3) In our culture, clinical psychologists and psychiatrists use a manual known as the Diagnostic Statistical Manual of Mental Disorders to diagnose a person's mental illness. What does this activity suggest about the accuracy of the Diagnostic Statistical Manual in diagnosing a person's mental illness, particularly if the person is from another culture?

References

Simons, R. C., and Hughes, C. C. 1993. Culture-bound syndromes. In A. C. Gaw (ed.), *Culture, Ethnicity and Mental Illness.* Washington, DC: American Psychiatric Press.

Weiten, W. 1998. *Psychology, themes and variations.* 4th ed. Pacific Grove, CA: Brooks-Cole.

Concept and Goal

This activity allows you to examine the barriers that occur in the therapy setting with minority patients and examine some solutions and strategies for overcoming these barriers. This is a small-group activity. In your group, you should develop solutions to the barriers for minorities in getting effective therapy. Each group should then present the responses and prepare the discussion questions for class interaction.

Instructions

Research on how cultural factors influence the process and outcome of psychotherapy has increased in recent years; this research has been motivated in part by the need to improve mental health services for ethnic minority groups in American society. Studies suggest that American minority groups generally underutilize therapeutic services (Mays & Albee, 1992). Weiten (1998) presents several barriers that exist in providing psychological therapy to minority group persons. Your instructor will assign you to a group of five to six students to develop solutions to and strategies for overcoming these barriers in counseling and treating minorities for psychological problems.

1. Cultural barriers. Given the socialization of many ethnic minorities, they prefer to rely on informal assistance from family members, the clergy, respected elders, herbalists, acupuncturists, and so on, who share their cultural heritage. Many members of minority groups have a history of frustrating interactions with American bureaucracies and are distrustful of large, intimidating, foreign institutions, such as hospitals and community mental health centers.

Solution:

2. Language barriers. Effective communication is crucial to providing psychotherapy, yet many hospitals and mental health agencies are not adequately staffed with therapists who speak the languages used by minority groups in their service areas. The resulting communication problems make it awkward and difficult for many minority group members to explain their problems and to obtain the type of help they need.

Solution:

3. Access barriers. Many minority groups suffer from high rates of joblessness and poverty. In our society, people who are unemployed or employed in economically marginal jobs typically do not have health insurance. Their lack of health insurance restricts their options in pursuing treatment for psychological problems.

Solution:

4. Institutional barriers. The vast majority of therapists are white middle-class Americans who have been trained almost exclusively in the treatment of white, middle-class American patients and are not familiar with the cultural backgrounds and unique characteristics of various ethnic groups. This cultural gap often leads to misunderstandings and poor treatment strategies for ethnic minority persons.

Solution:

Discussion Questions

1) Do you think a patient and therapist in a counseling setting should be of the same ethnic group? Same sex? Why or why not?

2) If you were working in a mental health center with a large minority population, what could you do in that community that might facilitate your success with your patients in the counseling setting?

References

Mays, V. M., and Albee, G. W. 1992. Psychotherapy and ethnic minorities. In D. K. Freedheim (ed.), *History of Psychotherapy: A Century of Change.* Washington, DC: American Psychological Association.

Weiten, W. 1998. *Psychology themes and variations.* 4th ed. Pacific Grove, CA: Brooks Cole.

Source: Activity from Weiten, W. 1998. *Psychology themes & variations.* 4th ed., 626. Pacific Grove, CA: Brooks Cole.

Activity

70

Just World

Concept and Goal

This activity allows you to examine the extent to which you believe in a just world. You should complete the scale and then prepare the discussion questions for class interaction.

Instructions

Melvin Lerner's (1974) just-world hypothesis states that we all need to believe in a just world in which people get what they deserve and conversely deserve what they get. Zick Rubin and Letitia Peplau developed the Just World Scale (JWS). Indicate your degree of agreement or disagreement with each of the following statements in the blank space next to each item. Respond to every statement by using the following scale.

0 - strongly disagree
1 - moderately disagree
2 - slightly disagree
3 - slightly agree
4 - moderately agree
5 - strongly agree

_____ 1. I have found that a person rarely deserves the reputation he has.

_____ 2. Basically, the world is a just place.

_____ 3. People who get "lucky breaks" have usually earned their good fortune.

_____ 4. Careful drivers are just as likely to get hurt in traffic accidents as careless ones.

_____ 5. It is a common occurrence for a guilty person to get off free in American courts.

_____ 6. Students almost always deserve the grades they receive in school.

_____ 7. Persons who keep in shape have little chance of suffering a heart attack.

_____ 8. The political candidate who sticks up for his principles rarely gets elected.

_____ 9. It is rare for an innocent person to be wrongly sent to jail.

_____ 10. In professional sports, many fouls and infractions never get called by the referee.

_____ 11. By and large, people deserve what they get.

_____ 12. When parents punish their children, it is almost always for good reasons.

_____ 13. Good deeds often go unnoticed and unrewarded.

_____ 14. Although evil persons may hold political power for a while, in the general course of

history good wins out.

_____ 15. In almost any business or profession, people who do their job will rise to the top.

_____ 16. American parents tend to overlook the things that should be most admired in their

children.

_____ 17. It is often impossible for a person to receive a fair trial in the U.S.

_____ 18. People who meet with misfortune have often brought it on themselves.

_____ 19. Crime doesn't pay.

_____ 20. Many people suffer through absolutely no fault of their own.

Scoring
1) Reverse individual scores on items 1, 4, 5, 8, 10, 13, 16, 17, 20 (change 0 to 5, 1 to 4, 2 to 3, 3 to 2, 4 to 1, and 5 to 0 for the questions).
2) Add the numbers in front of all 20 items.

Total scores can range from 0 to 100, with higher scores indicating a stronger belief in a just world and lower scores indicating little belief in a just world. For comparison purposes, scores of Boston University undergraduates were slightly below the midpoint, whereas those of Oklahoma State University students were slightly above the midpoint.

Discussion Questions
1) Did the results of your score indicate that you believe in a just world? Explain.

2) How can a belief in a just world possibly create prejudice against disadvantaged groups?

3) Research indicates that people with certain characteristics have a strong belief in a just world. What type of people do you think fall into this category?

4) What type of people do not have a strong belief in a just world? Explain why.

References
    Lerner, M. J. 1974. Social psychology of justice and interpersonal attraction. In T. Huston (ed.), *Foundations of Interpersonal Attraction.* New York: Academic Press.
    Rubin, Z., and Peplau, L. A. 1975. Who believes in a just world. *Journal of Social Issues* 31: 65–89.

Activity
71

Personal Space

Concept and Goal

This activity demonstrates the concept of personal space. Research indicates that there are cultural and gender differences in personal space, and personal space is one nonverbal cue that regulates intimacy in interpersonal relationships. This is a class activity. After the class has completed the activity, you should prepare the discussion questions for class interaction.

Instructions

The instructor will provide instructions to carry out this activity on personal space.

Discussion Questions

1) What were your subjective experiences during the activity? Why do you think you had those experiences?

2) Do you think groups of people differ in the personal space boundaries they find appropriate when interacting with others (e.g., men, women, North Americans, Africans, Latin-Americans, Arabs, etc.)? If groups differ, what do you think the nature of the differences are?

3) What can be the effect when people with different personal space norms interact together?

References

Gibson, B., Harris, P., and Werner, C. 1993. Intimacy and personal space: A classroom demonstration. *Teaching of Psychology* 20: 180–181.

Hall, E. T. 1966. *The hidden dimension.* New York: Doubleday.

Patterson, M. 1977. Interpersonal distance, affect, and equilibrium theory. *Journal of Social Psychology* 101: 205–214.

Tennis, G., and Dabbs, J. 1975. Sex, setting and personal space: First grade through college. *Sociometry* 38: 385–394.

Source: Activity by Gibson, B., Harris, P., and Werner, C. 1993. Intimacy and personal space: A classroom demonstration. *Teaching of Psychology* 20: 180–181.

End-of-the-World Stereotyping

Concept and Goal

This activity allows you to examine your own stereotypes and relate them to research on stereotype theory and compliance in group situations. This is a small-group activity.

Instructions

Read the following passage from Goodman's article from the *Activities Handbook for the Teaching of Psychology* (1981), and answer discussion question 1. You will then be assigned to a small-group to answer questions 1–4; for question 1 you should come to a group consensus. Each group should then discuss and present the responses to all the questions for class interaction.

End of the World

Imagine that our country is under threat of imminent nuclear attack. A person approaches you and asks you to make an independent decision concerning a nearby fallout shelter that can accommodate 6 people but has 12 people vying to get in. Based on the following information about the 12 people, which 6 would you choose to go in the shelter? The group includes a 40-year-old male violinist who is a suspected narcotics pusher; a 34-year-old male architect who is thought be a homosexual; a 26-year-old lawyer and the lawyer's 24-year-old wife who has just gotten out of a mental institution—they both want to go in together or stay out together; a 75-year-old priest; a 34-year-old retired prostitute who was so successful that she's been living off her annuities for five years; a 20-year-old black militant; a 23-year-old female graduate student who has had several bouts of depression throughout her life; a 28-year-old physicist who will only come into the shelter if he can bring his gun with him; a 30-year-old female medical doctor who is an avowed bigot; a 12-year-old girl who has a low IQ; and a male who has been deaf since birth.

Discussion Questions

1) Which six people should be allowed in the fallout shelter? What factors were most important to you in determining who should be protected in the fallout shelter? Explain why those factors were most important?

2) In the group consensus discussion, did you stand up for what you believed?

3) Did you feel pressure to conform? If so, who or what caused it?

4) How did you reach group decisions? Did you feel part of those decisions?

References

Allport, G. W. 1954. *The nature of prejudice.* Reading, MA: Addison-Wesley.

Campbell, D. T. 1967. Stereotypes and the perception of group differences. *American Psychologist* 22: 817–829.

Cialdini, R. 1993. *Influence: Science and practice.* Boston: Addison Wesley Longman.

Goodman, J. 1981. Group decisions and stereotypes. In L. Benjamin and K. Lowman (eds.), *Activities Handbook for the Teaching of Psychology.* Washington, DC: American Psychological Association.

Tajfel, H. 1963. Stereotypes. *Race* 5: 3–14.

Activity

73

Perceptions of Sexism

Concept and Goal

This activity examines if there are gender differences in the perceptions of sexism in social situations. This is a class activity. Students will individually have adults rate the scenarios in the handout. The class will analyze and discuss the results and the discussion questions.

Instructions

Though it is undesirable to be sexist, research shows that individuals continue to exhibit sexism. One possible reason for this discrepancy is that there is significant disagreement as to what constitutes sexism. This activity presents eight scenarios of possible sexism (Handout 1). Give these eight scenarios to a group of adults (approximately half female and half male) and ask them to rate the scenarios for the extent of sexism.

Your instructor will give you instructions to complete the activity.

Discussion Questions

1) Did the results from your class's data indicate that males and females differ in their perceptions of sexism?

2) If gender differences were found, what do these results indicate about relationships between males and females?

3) If gender differences were found, what do these results indicate about eliminating sex discrimination in our society?

4) If gender differences were not found, give possible reasons why.

5) Do you think that males and females would differ in their perceptions of sexism in a culture where exploitation and abuse of women is not viewed as wrong, as it is in the U.S.? Explain.

References

Ho, C. 1990. An analysis of domestic violence in Asian American communities: A multicultural approach to counseling. *Women and Therapy* 9: 129–150.

Pryor, J. B., DeSouza, E. R., Fitness, J., Hutz, C., Kumpf, M., Lubbert, K., Pesonen, O., and Erber, M. W. 1997. Gender differences in the interpretation of social-sexual behavior. *Journal of Cross-Cultural Psychology* 28: 509–534.

Smith, E. R. 1992. Differential perceptions of sexism. *Women & Therapy* 12: 187–200.

Handout 1

Read each of the eight scenarios and rate the degree of sexism on a scale from 1 (definitely is not) to 7 (definitely is).

1. Amy asks Richard out to dinner and he accepts. At the end of the meal, she tries to pay the check but he insists on paying it, telling her that the man should always pay the check. Is Richard being sexist?

1	2	3	4	5	6	7
Definitely is not						Definitely is

2. Stephanie has noticed that when she goes to a restaurant with a group of friends, people seem to feel uncomfortable if she raises her voice. Is it sexist to disapprove of Stephanie raising her voice?

1	2	3	4	5	6	7
Definitely is not						Definitely is

3. Adrianne worked in public relations. She was fired when she told her boss that she was pregnant. He said her image as a pregnant woman would not correspond to the image the company wants to project. Was her boss being sexist?

1	2	3	4	5	6	7
Definitely is not						Definitely is

4. Dr. Bowling is a professor who received the comment from her students that she should smile more while lecturing. None of her male colleagues has ever received such a comment. Were her students making a sexist comment?

1	2	3	4	5	6	7
Definitely is not						Definitely is

5. Sue is pregnant and will be having a baby in two months. She asked her boss if she could take an unpaid maternity leave for four months. Her boss responds no, the company is too busy. Is Sue's boss being sexist?

1	2	3	4	5	6	7
Definitely is not						Definitely is

6. Kathy is on a date with Roger. Roger makes a point of opening all the doors for Kathy. Kathy tells Roger that is not necessary, she prefers to do this herself. However, Roger continues to open the door for Kathy. Is Roger being sexist?

1	2	3	4	5	6	7
Definitely is not						Definitely is

7. Mary has gotten married. She decides to retain her maiden name. Her husband wants her to assume his surname. Mary refuses and her husband gets angry. He can't understand why Mary wants to retain her maiden name. Is Mary's husband being sexist?

1	2	3	4	5	6	7
Definitely is not						Definitely is

8. Joe and Denise were hired at the same time for the same level position. They both have similar educational backgrounds and work experiences. However, Joe's salary is $2,000 more than Denise's. Is the owner who hired them being sexist?

1	2	3	4	5	6	7
Definitely is not						Definitely is

Data Worksheet

Sex _____ M   _____ F

Scenario 1 score _____
Scenario 2 score _____
Scenario 3 score _____
Scenario 4 score _____
Scenario 5 score _____
Scenario 6 score _____
Scenario 7 score _____
Scenario 8 score _____

For each participant, add scores for the eight scenarios and compute a mean

Male participants' mean scores _____   Female participants' mean scores _____

Activity

74

Sex-Role Behaviors

Concept and Goal

This activity demonstrates how thoroughly sex-role perceptions influence our behavior without our awareness. This is a small-group activity. You should read the passage on body politics individually, and your group should discuss this passage together. The focus of the discussion should be on the following issues: (1) your reactions to the assertions in the reading, (2) sexism as you experience it or don't experience it, and (3) how your group would go about testing the validity of the assertions made in the reading. The instructor will then present data to you based on your discussion, and your group should prepare the discussion questions for class interaction.

Instructions

Read the following material from Nancy Henley's *Body Politics* (1977). Your instructor will then assign you to a group and your group should discuss various issues based on the passage.

During the course of the book, *Body Politics*, Henley attempts to put forward and document the following points:

1. Nonverbal behavior is a major medium of communication in our everyday life.
2. Power (status, dominance) is expressed through nonverbal communication; and thus nonverbal communication is a major avenue for social control.
3. Nonverbal control is of particular importance to women, who are more sensitive to its cues and probably more often the targets of such control.
4. The behaviors expressing dominance and subordination between equals and nonequals parallel those used by males and females in the unequal relation of the sexes.

Based on the evidence, Henley develops the following table, summarizing nonverbal behaviors used between equals (intimate and nonintimate), nonequals (superior and subordinate), and men and women.

		Between Status Equals Intimate (Nonintimate)	Between Status Nonequals Used by Superior (Used by Subordinate)	Between Men and Women Used by Men (Used by Women)
	Gestures of Power and Privilege **Examples of Some Nonverbal Behaviors with Usage Differing for** **Status Equals, Status Nonequals, and for Women and Men**			
1.	Address	Familiar (Polite)	Familiar (Polite)	Familiar (Polite)
2.	Demeanor	Informal (Circumspect)	Informal (Circumspect)	Informal (Circumspect)
3.	Posture	Relaxed (Tense)	Relaxed (Tense)	Relaxed (Tense)
4.	Personal Space	Closeness (Distance)	Closeness (Distance)	Closeness (Distance)
5.	Time	Long (Short)	Long (Short)	Long (Short)
6.	Touching	Touch (Don't touch)	Touch (Don't touch)	Touch (Don't touch)

From this table, it can be seen that the six nonverbal behavior categories show completely parallel structure when comparing the top row to the bottom row for each column; the form used between intimates is used to inferiors and women and the form used between nonintimates is used to superiors and men.

Discussion Questions
1) Did your group behave in gender stereotypical ways during the class discussion of Henley's book? If so, how were gender differences in your group's behavior similar to or different from Henley's work on sex differences in nonverbal behavior?

2) If your group did not behave in gender stereotypical ways during the class discussion of Henley's book, give possible reasons why.

3) Did you feel deceived since you did not know that your behavior was being observed during the group discussion? Discuss the role of ethics in social psychological research—should deception occur and under what circumstances?

References

Bales, R. 1950. *Interaction process analysis.* Reading, MA: Wesley.

Bardwick, J. 1971. *Psychology of women: A study of biocultural conflicts.* New York: Harper & Row.

Cole, D. 1981. Sexism in the classroom. In L. Benjamin and K. Lowman (eds.), *Activities Handbook for the Teaching of Psychology.* Washington, DC: American Psychological Association.

Guttentag, M., and Bray, H. 1976. *Undoing sex stereotypes.* New York: McGraw-Hill.

Henley, N. 1977. *Body politics: Power, sex and nonverbal communication.* Englewood Cliffs, NJ: Prentice-Hall.

Activity 75

Magazine Portrayals

Concept and Goal

This activity demonstrates the pervasiveness of gender stereotypes in the mass media using Goffman's (1976) categorization of subtle stereotyping. You should answer the items individually, but the class should review and discuss the answers and discussion questions.

Materials

Your instructor will present you with 20 slides from advertisements from earlier magazines (1950s) and current magazines.

Instructions

Your instructor will explain Goffman's research on subtle stereotyping. You will be asked by your instructor which of Goffman's genderisms is portrayed in the slides that he or she presents. As you view each slide, use the data worksheet and circle the gender theme(s) depicted in each slide.

Discussion Questions

1) Describe your perceptions of the gender stereotyping in the advertisements as you viewed them.

2) Use your imagination and change the sex of the models. Do the pictures seem natural? Why or why not?

3) What are the similarities in the portrayals of men and women in today's advertisements compared to those of the 1950s?

4) What are the differences in the portrayals of men and women in today's advertisements compared to those of the 1950s?

References

Goffman, E. 1976. *Gender advertisements.* New York: Harper & Row.

Jones, M. 1991. Gender stereotyping in advertisements. *Teaching of Psychology* 18: 231–233.

Source: Activity by Jones, M. 1991. Gender stereotyping in advertisements. *Teaching of Psychology* 18: 231–233.

Data Worksheet

Function ranking (FR)
Relative size (RS)
Ritualization of subordination (RiS)
Feminine touch (FT)
Family (F)

Circle the appropriate genderism(s).

Ad 1	FR	RS	RiS	FT	F	N/A
Ad 2	FR	RS	RiS	FT	F	N/A
Ad 3	FR	RS	RiS	FT	F	N/A
Ad 4	FR	RS	RiS	FT	F	N/A
Ad 5	FR	RS	RiS	FT	F	N/A
Ad 6	FR	RS	RiS	FT	F	N/A
Ad 7	FR	RS	RiS	FT	F	N/A
Ad 8	FR	RS	RiS	FT	F	N/A
Ad 9	FR	RS	RiS	FT	F	N/A
Ad 10	FR	RS	RiS	FT	F	N/A
Ad 11	FR	RS	RiS	FT	F	N/A
Ad 12	FR	RS	RiS	FT	F	N/A
Ad 13	FR	RS	RiS	FT	F	N/A
Ad 14	FR	RS	RiS	FT	F	N/A
Ad 15	FR	RS	RiS	FT	F	N/A
Ad 16	FR	RS	RiS	FT	F	N/A
Ad 17	FR	RS	RiS	FT	F	N/A
Ad 18	FR	RS	RiS	FT	F	N/A
Ad 19	FR	RS	RiS	FT	F	N/A
Ad 20	FR	RS	RiS	FT	F	N/A

Activity

76

Blaming Behaviors

Concept and Goal

This activity sensitizes you to the tendency among many of us to blame the victim. Also, the implications of this phenomenon are explored.

Instructions

Read the following passage from Dolgoff and Feldstein's *Understanding Social Welfare* (1984) and complete the exercise at the end of the passage and the discussion questions.

Who is to Blame?

Once upon a time, a husband and a wife lived together in a part of the city separated by a river from the places of employment, shopping, and entertainment. The husband had to work nights. Each evening he left his wife and took the ferry to work, returning in the morning.

The wife soon tired of this arrangement. Restless and lonely, she would take the next ferry into town and develop relationships with a series of lovers. Anxious to preserve her marriage, she always returned home before her husband. In fact, her relationships were always limited. When they threatened to become too intense, she would precipitate a quarrel with her current lover and begin a new relationship.

One night she caused such a quarrel with a man we will call Lover 1. He slammed the door in her face, and she started back to the ferry. Suddenly she realized that she had forgotten to bring money for her return fare. She swallowed her pride and returned to Lover 1's apartment. But Lover 1 was vindictive and angry because of the quarrel. He slammed the door on his former lover, leaving her with no money. She remembered that a previous lover, who we shall call Lover 2, lived just a few doors away. Surely he would give her the ferry fare. However, Lover 2 was still so hurt from their old quarrel that he, too, refused her the money.

Now the hour was late and the woman was getting desperate. She rushed down to the ferry and pleaded with the ferryboat captain. He knew her as a regular customer. She asked if he could let her ride free and if she could pay the next night. But the captain insisted that rules were rules and that he could not let her ride without paying the fare.

Dawn would soon be breaking, and her husband would be returning from work. The woman remembered that there was a free bridge about a mile further on. But the road to the bridge was a dangerous one, known to be frequented by highwaymen. Nonetheless, she had to get home, so she took the road. On the way, a highwayman stepped out of the buses and demanded her money. She told him she had none. He seized her. In the ensuing tussle, the highwayman stabbed the woman, and she died.

Thus ends our story. There have been six characters: Husband, Wife, Lover 1, Lover 2, Ferryboat Captain, and Highwayman. Please list, in descending order of responsibility for this woman's death, all the characters. In other words, the one most responsible is listed first, the next most responsible, second, and so forth.

Most responsible
    First:
    Second:
    Third:
    Fourth:
    Fifth:
    Sixth:
Least responsible

Discussion Questions

1) Who do you think is most often blamed for the woman's death in this passage? Why?

2) Can you think of groups of victims in our society who tend to get blamed for their circumstances?

3) In the subfield of social psychology, there is a theory known as the actor-observer bias. The actor-observer bias states that actors and observers make different attributions about the causes of the actor's behavior. An observer attributes an actor's behavior to the internal qualities of the actor, but the actor attributes his or her own behavior to external factors affecting her or him. How does blaming the victim in this exercise support the actor-observer bias?

References

Bloyd, J. R. October 1990. *Blaming the victim.* Presented at the Mid-America Conference for Teachers of Psychology, Evansville, IN.

Dolgoff, R., and Feldstein, D. 1984. *Understanding social welfare.* 2nd ed. New York: Longman.

Source: Activity by Dolgoff, R., and Feldstein, D. 1984. *Understanding social welfare.* 2nd ed., 1–4. New York: Longman.

Activity 77

Cultural Incidents

Concept and Goal

This activity examines the cultural differences in the desirability of particular behaviors in social situations. You will understand the nature of culture as well as prepare to interact effectively with people from different cultural groups. This is a small-group activity.

Instructions

Brislin and his colleagues (1986) have prepared a collection of 100 critical incidents. Panels of experts wrote the incidents, which were reviewed and edited by panels composed of citizens of the portrayed country and also ex-sojourners who had worked or traveled for extended periods in the targeted country. We are presenting one incident from each of Brislin et al.'s eight settings: host customs, interacting with hosts, settling in and making adjustments, tourist experiences, the workplace, the family, education and schooling, and returning home. Read each incident. After each incident, you will be asked a question. Select the option that seems to best answer the question. The answer to the question is then given along with explanations. After your group has checked its answers, the group should prepare the discussion questions for class interaction.

1—Host Customs
Eating Out in Brazil

Two Americans visiting Brazil on business were taken by their hosts to lunch at a restaurant. When everyone was seated, the waitress put down one menu in the middle of the table for all four people, the two Americans and two Brazilians. The Americans were surprised that they did not each receive a menu, but the Brazilians did not seem perturbed. One of the Americans asked the waitress why she did not give everyone a menu. Without batting an eye she said, "they are all the same"—and left the table.

The Americans resignedly looked at the one menu and memorized their selections, muttering to each other about the rudeness of the waitress and the cheapness of the restaurant. The Brazilians seemed to accept the situation matter-of-factly.

Why did the waitress give them only one menu?
(1)   It was a deliberate snub on the part of the waitress, who disliked the sometimes arrogant attitude of American tourists.
(2)   It was a cheap restaurant and there simply were not enough menus to go around.
(3)   The waitress assumed the Americans would not understand the Brazilian menu, and so did not bother providing extra copies for them.
(4)   Brazilians do not really see the need for individual menus.

Key for Incident 1

(1)　There is no indication that this is the case. Brazilians generally do not have strong anti-American attitudes, and the waitress is more likely to be concerned with earning a larger tip than deliberately upsetting the Americans.

(2)　There is no indication that this is so, and it is unlikely that the Brazilians would take American acquaintances to very low-class restaurants. (In such restaurants there is quite likely to be no menu and one simply asks what is available to eat.)

(3)　The waitress would probably check with the Americans or their Brazilian hosts before making such an assumption. There is a more probable explanation.

(4)　This is the best alternative. Brazilians are more group-oriented than individualistic Americans. As such they are more likely to make decisions such as ordering on a group basis or leaving it up to the senior person or host to make suggestions as to what they should have. One menu will thus suffice, and the waitress would not understand the need for more copies of the same menu.

2—Interacting with Hosts
Social Ease

Daureen was thrilled to have been asked by some of her new friends at school to attend a birthday party in honor of one of the girls' sisters. She had only recently arrived in Indonesia from the United States as part of a student exchange program and was excited to be meeting new friends.

When she arrived at the party, she found many new things to experience. The food was certainly different, the drinks seemed to taste strange, and even the birthday greeting was done in a way she was not accustomed to. She was even aware that she was the only one dressed in typically Western clothes. This made her feel uneasy as she had gone to a lot of trouble to look her best. It didn't seem right that she should feel so awkward. She didn't seem to know how to act appropriately. She began feeling more and more uneasy as the night wore on.

Deciding that perhaps some food would help to relax her, Daureen approached a food table and began to help herself. Upon leaving the table, she inadvertently tripped on the leg of a chair and spilled her drink on the floor. Immediately, one of the girls nearby stooped down to begin mopping up the spill and everyone else in the room began laughing out loud. Daureen, uncertain of what to do next, quietly moved out of the way with her head lowered in shame. She kept to herself for the remainder of the evening, hoping to avoid more trouble.

What is a good explanation of the reaction to the spilled drink in this incident?

(1)　Daureen had obviously been acting in an inappropriate manner all evening. The spilling of the drink was the straw that broke the camel's back, so to speak. Everyone simply found her actions amusing and could hold the laughter back no longer.

(2)　Laughter is a means to disperse tension in Indonesia.

(3)　Daureen began the evening wrong by not bringing a gift to the host. This immediately put the others against her; thus the above incident.

(4)　Daureen is experiencing a major form of culture shock. The laughter is probably not due to anything she did.

Key for Incident 2

(1)   Although Daureen did look and act differently from the others around her, this would not explain the apparent ridicule. Indonesians are characteristically accepting of most people.

(2)   This is the most correct answer. In Indonesia, laughter is one means to disperse a tense, embarrassing, or otherwise difficult situation. It tells others that one is cared for and that they will help lessen your burden by sharing it and lightening it. Even when talking about the death of a close friend or relative, others may laugh, again to help disperse the tears and lighten the burden.

(3)   Although in Indonesia it is appropriate to bring a gift to your host, this is not what led to the behavior focused on here.

(4)   This answer, while quite possible, is not fully correct. Appeals to the general reaction of culture shock are not as helpful as understanding the exact reasons for people's behavior. The laughter was triggered by the spilled drink. The best answer focuses on the meaning of the laughter.

3—Settling In and Making Adjustments
A Pacific Paradise?

Barbara had been teaching in Samoa for about three months when she became aware of an increasing uneasiness. She had made a remarkable adjustment at first, or so she thought. All the excitement when she arrived, the people who came to greet her, the peering faces as she set up home, those interested in her work at the school, and the freedom with which people came to visit her home, all made her feel welcome. All this contact continued.

She was surprised at how well she took to the new foods, daily patterns, and change of activities, especially because this was her first real teaching job since she graduated from college. She was learning the new language at a reasonable rate. She felt respected in her school and was confident that she was well liked, both by professional peers and by those in the community. People were always coming to her home. Everyone seemed to be looking out for her.

Everything seemed right, at least on the outside. Yet, she was aware of becoming increasingly anxious, irritated, self-conscious, and, in a sense, paranoid, all without any apparent reason.

What is a good explanation for Barbara's recent reaction to her experiences?

(1)   This is Barbara's reaction to the lack of privacy afforded her.

(2)   This is Barbara's disappointment that things didn't shock her system upon her arrival. She felt as if some part of the adjustment process was not occurring as it was supposed to.

(3)   This is Barbara's latent reaction to having a routine job.

(4)   This is Barbara's reaction to a lack of close friends.

Key for Incident 3

(1)   While Barbara sees all the contact she has with people constantly watching her as a sign of acceptance, it is very possible that she is reacting to the lack of privacy. Samoans typically include themselves in much of another's life and business. Houses have no walls and so Barbara's standards of privacy, based on closed doors, was not workable in Samoa. Although

this is a signal that Barbara has been accepted by members of the community, it also opens the door (so to speak) to a lack of privacy to which she is not accustomed. This is the best answer.

(2) While most sojourners expect to have some adjustment difficulties and Barbara did not report any, it is unlikely that she would have the feelings and react the way she is reported to as a result of this.

(3) Although this is Barbara's first real job, there is no indication in the incident that she is finding it difficult to adjust to her teaching. To the contrary, she feels quite confident in her work.

(4) Although a lack of close friends is often a critical factor in one's satisfactory adjustment to a new culture, and there is no mention of friends in the incident, Barbara would not be reporting these feelings as a result of this.

4—Tourist Experiences
A Political Debate?

Sharlene and Qing-yu were discussing an assignment for their political science class, looking at the differences in policies held by various countries. They decided it would be easier to talk about their own countries first and then compare them. As Sharlene was expounding upon the international policies of the United States, Qing-yu asked her about an aspect that she thought illogical and did not quite understand. Sharlene agreed that it did not make any sense, and then began stating several other such policies, as well as her criticisms of them. Qing-yu was very surprised, but made no comment. Later as Qing-yu was explaining several Chinese policies, Sharlene interrupted with a comment, and proceeded to list her objections and criticisms to several other related policies. Qing-yu became quite defensive and upset and finally refused to continue any further discussion and left.

How would you help explain Qing-yu's behavior?
(1) Qing-yu did not understand much about politics and was confused by Sharlene's train of thoughts.
(2) Qing-yu felt that Sharlene was attacking her personally.
(3) Qing-yu did not like being interrupted and felt that Sharlene was being very rude.
(4) Qing-yu had a much more ethnocentric view of her country's policies than Sharlene and thus was offended.

Key for Incident 4

(1) Since both Qing-yu and Sharlene were in the political science class together, we can assume that they were both academically on the same level. Even if this were not so, most Chinese scholars that are studying abroad are very versed on their country's policies and politics. There is nothing in the incident to indicate that Sharlene confused her.

(2) Often when people speak about things that reflect part of us (certainly in terms of country or nationality), we take it personally, even though it is not meant to be so. Although Qing-yu may have felt somewhat personally berated, Sharlene's comments were pertaining to political policies and views and should not be taken personally. This is partially correct, but there is a better answer.

(3)   No one likes to be interrupted. However, it does not appear that Sharlene did this in a rude fashion nor that she cut off Qing-yu's opinion; it would seem more of an interjection. There is another factor offending Qing-yu.

(4)   In many Asian countries the citizens have a much more nationalistic world view than found in Western countries. They not only think very highly of their own country, but they also reserve the right to criticize it in their own limited way. That is, they will not allow others to find fault with their beloved homeland, which in their understanding cannot be compared with other countries. It is not that they do not really have a realistic view of the country, rather, that with respect to the rest of the world, they may have a colored viewpoint. China, in particular, has long held a viewpoint of superiority. In recent times, this has diminished somewhat, yet it still maintains a high degree of respect and loyalty from its citizens. Qing-yu, raised with these sorts of ideas, finds it hard to believe that Sharlene would berate her own country, but even more intolerable that she would openly criticize Qing-yu's, especially since it is one as great as China. Sharlene, in contrast, has been educated to question and analyze, considering both negative and positive aspects. Most countries cultivate some degree of ethnocentric thinking in their citizens, so every person has a tendency to think of their own homeland as wonderful. However, certain countries tolerate to a greater degree criticisms or varying opinions.

5—The Workplace
A Development Place

Having recently overseen the completion of the project that originally brought him to Africa, Matt was proud of the three years he had spent in Nigeria. He was able to acquire excellent materials for the sewage treatment system of which he was in charge. It was functioning well and was an important point of interest for various officials who visited Nigeria to report on the development process. Nigerian officials also pointed with pride to the sewage treatment system. Matt returned to Canada, the country whose technical assistance program sent him to Nigeria, with a promotion and a reputation for getting things done.

However, after five years, the sewage treatment system was not functioning well. Parts had rusted, and no one seemed able to replace worn out parts and to look after system maintenance. Officials in Nigeria, when asked to speak about the successful and unsuccessful development projects, stopped mentioning the sewage treatment system. Hosts did not report favorable retrospective feelings about Matt's three-year assignment in Nigeria.

What is the source of the problem with the sewage treatment system?

(1)   Matt was not able to use the best materials available. Eventually, these materials wore out.

(2)   Matt had not trained Nigerians in the skills necessary to carry on the work at the sewage treatment system.

(3)   The hosts resented the development assistance from Canada since this put Nigeria in the embarrassing role of the recipient of aid from outside.

(4)   Matt was careless in the details of construction, so what looked like a model sewage treatment system had many problems visible only to other construction engineers given unlimited rights of inspection.

Key for Incident 5

(1)   The story specifically says that Matt was able to acquire excellent materials. Just because materials wear out, this does not mean that Matt has used inadequate materials. Maintenance, including the replacement of worn out parts, is part of the long-range success of any construction project.

(2)   This is the best answer. Matt may have done an excellent job in supervising construction of the system, but he did not transfer his skills to Nigerian hosts, especially skills concerned with maintenance. Research coming out of the Canadian International Development Agency has shown that transfer of skills is one of the major components of the long-range success of technical assistance advisers. Hosts are sensitive to the problem. In their own judgments concerning who are good versus poor sojourners, they incorporate observations of who (e.g., Matt) makes sure or does not make sure that hosts learn technical skills that allow maintenance of the current project and construction of others. The conclusion from this research is that excellent training and experience in engineering is not enough. Technical assistants must also have enough human relation skills, and cultural knowledge, to be able to develop procedures by which hosts learn engineering skills from the sojourner(s).

(3)   Although occasionally this is a problem, it is not widespread enough to constitute an answer to why the sewage treatment system became nonfunctioning. If this answer is chosen, the reasoning would be that host resentment caused purposeful sabotage. But the story indicated that Nigerians were proud of the project. They would not be expected to sabotage something they valued, even if they were not completely happy with the source of the sewage treatment system.

(4)   There is no evidence to suggest this is the case. Matt was known to be a good engineer, was proud of his work, and from all accounts left Nigeria to return to Canada leaving behind an excellent piece of construction. Just because the system developed problems, this does not mean that the original construction was poor. Careful maintenance is necessary for the smooth functioning of any complex project.

6—The Family
Heading Up Operations in the Mideast

George Lefferts had been a mid-level manager for a petroleum firm headquartered in Dallas, Texas, for 20 years. During the last few years, he had become increasingly disillusioned with his position with the company. It became more and more apparent that he had reached the highest position he would reach with them. He wanted more out of life.

His relationship with his wife, too, had soured over the past few years. He and his wife Helen grew increasingly impatient with each other. They were unsure of what they wanted from their marriage and from their lives together now that their children had grown and were gone.

A sudden opportunity to head up operations for two years in a Middle Eastern country was received enthusiastically by both George and Helen. This seemed to be the spark that excited them about their future together. Both actively involved themselves in language and cultural preparation for the three months prior to their departure. Together they went shopping for items they thought they would want with them, cleared out some of the unneeded goods from their home, and began frequenting Middle Eastern restaurants in Dallas. They even arranged to rent their home and were pleased with the tenant they got.

The overseas adjustment was initially difficult, but they had faith that everything would go well. Others at work and in the housing compound assured them that they, too, would successfully adapt to the local conditions. But, although their use of the local language and their ease at living and adapting to local conditions improved, their interactions in their home rapidly deteriorated. Within four months of arrival, they asked to be transferred back home.

What major issue is the cause of their problem?
(1)   Losing contact with their family and fellow countrymen was too difficult to adjust to.
(2)   Preexisting interpersonal difficulties resurfaced.
(3)   George was still uneasy with his standing in the company and would probably remain so until this issue was addressed.
(4)   George should not have listened to the advice of the others in the compound regarding his adjustment. He should have acted earlier to alleviate any problems.

Key for Incident 6
(1)   Helen and George had already separated from their family. Also, the housing compound is presumably shared with fellow countrymen and certainly is shared with other English speakers. There is a more pressing issue at play here.
(2)   Interpersonal tensions existed before their move. Although the excitement of the move seemed to bring Helen and George together again, this was only temporary. The root of their problem had never been addressed and was certain to resurface again once the move was made, only stronger this time because of the compounding effects of the new influences around them. A sudden change, although apparently exciting at first, only temporarily masked deep problems. These should have been fully addressed prior to any big move. Compounding the situation is the fact that George and Helen would tend to spend a considerably greater amount of time with each other without the contact of friends and others. This is the best answer.
(3)   It is unlikely that this is the root of the problem at hand. By accepting this new position, George has in effect already improved his position with the company. There is a much better response.
(4)   To the contrary, seeking the advice and guidance of others who had experienced similar changes is often helpful in that it sets the framework of expectations one can anticipate and prepare for. Knowing that others experience similar reactions tends to make the transition much easier.

7—Education and Schooling
Informal Gatherings of People
After a year in the United States, Fumio, from Japan, seemed to be adjusting well to his graduate-level studies. He had cordial relations with his professors, interacted frequently with other graduate students at midday coffee breaks, and was content with his housing arrangements in the graduate student dormitory. Fumio's statistical knowledge was so good that professors recommended that certain

American students consult him for help in this area. He seemed to be excluded, however, from at least one type of activity in which many of the other American graduate students participated. This was the informal gatherings of students at the local pub at about 5:00 on Friday afternoons. People did not stop and invite him to these gatherings. Since he was not invited, Fumio felt uncomfortable about simply showing up at the pub. Fumio wondered if the lack of an invitation should be interpreted as a sign that he was doing something wrong—and he was offending the American students in some way.

What is a good analysis of the situation involving the lack of invitation to the pub gatherings?

(1)   The Americans were rude in not inviting Fumio, a guest in their country.

(2)   The pub gatherings are meant to be an activity in which people who are very familiar with each other (an in-group) can relax on a very informal basis.

(3)   Japanese rarely drink beer. Realizing this, the Americans did not invite Fumio.

(4)   The Americans resented the fact that Fumio knew more statistics than they did, and this made the Americans feel inferior because they had to ask Fumio for help.

(5)   Pub gatherings on Friday afternoons, like this one, are largely based on pairings of specific males with specific females (or vice versa). Because Fumio had no girlfriend, he was not invited.

Key for Incident 7

(1)   While in an ideal world people would be extremely sensitive to each other and make sure of invitations to participants in such gatherings, people's busy schedules mean that social niceties are not followed to the ultimate level. It is doubtful that the Americans wanted to be rude; and the nature of the Friday afternoon gatherings is such that the Americans might have felt that Fumio would have been uncomfortable if he actually participated.

(2)   This is the best answer. There are often activities within a culture that are meant for the in-group, a number of people very familiar with each other and with whom everyone feels comfortable. The purpose of the gatherings is relaxation: People tell jokes based on shared experiences in the culture, do not have to impress each other since they already are familiar with the group's members, and generally relieve tension after a busy week. Fumio would interfere slightly with these purposes. He would not be able to understand the points of the jokes, he is not well-enough known to everyone to contribute to the relaxed atmosphere, and so on. Good questions to ask on a sojourn are, "Are there activities in which only in-group members regularly participate? How often do these include sojourners, even those sojourners in a country for more than two or three years? If there are such activities, is it realistic for me to be insulted if I am not included?"

(3)   The Japanese make some of the finest beer in the world and many enjoy its consumption.

(4)   While jealousy of a good-performing colleague is always a possibility, ill-feelings of American graduate students toward those from other countries is not common enough to constitute a likely explanation here. Just because the Americans ask for help does not mean that they will be resentful of the help received.

(5)   Friday afternoon gatherings of this type are not necessarily (or even frequently) based on

specific pairings of males and females. The fact that Fumio has no girlfriend is irrelevant.

8—Returning Home
Coming Back Home

Becky Engle had been home in Colorado for two months now, and she often found herself thinking of her time in the Philippines and wishing she were there. This confused her, as when she was there she had so longed to be home. She had despised the hot sticky weather in the Philippines and dreamed of the snows of the Rockies. The foods that the Filipino people ate she thought strange and untasty. She had often yearned for the fresh vegetables and salads of her native home in Boulder. There were countless things she had perpetually gone over that had annoyed her in the Philippines—the dirty air, the transportation system, the plumbing, and so on.

Now she was home, but the things she had missed about home while in the Philippines did not seem so important. What's more, she felt odd and out of place somehow and longed for the familiar things of her three years in the Philippines.

How could you help explain to Becky what is going on? Focus on her current feelings. Take into account as much information as possible.

(1)   Becky is going through a period of readjustment and feels that although things should seem familiar now, they are not.

(2)   Things in the Philippines were not as bad as she had imagined them and she was realizing that.

(3)   Becky is missing some of her friends in the Philippines. This is normal and she will get over it in a few months.

(4)   Becky had changed so much in her stay in the Philippines that she will no longer fit into her own society.

Key for Incident 8

(1)   Whenever there is change, adjustment is needed. One of the most problematic aspects of a sojourn is the fact that people often fail to realize that there will be difficulties readjusting to their original society. This is especially true when a longer period of time is spent on the sojourn. We spend much time and energy in preparing for the initial change and shock to a foreign or different society and presume that a return to our original starting place will not require any adjustments—because after all, we were brought up in that original place. We fail to acknowledge that the adjustments we have made to that other society have left us changed persons and certain other readjustments must be made to once again fit into the original mold. It is strange to think that things that should seem so familiar and comforting may actually make one uncomfortable. The fact is that sojourners change. They are still a part of their original cultural environment, but now have the addition of factors from another environment. The readjustment to original environments is termed re-entry shock. This is the best answer.

(2)   It is true that when things are not familiar, people tend to overemphasize or even to exaggerate factors out of the proper perspective. The discomforting factors in Becky's experience were real, however, and though they may have been somewhat exaggerated in her mind at the time of the experience and may have diminished in significance now, this does not explain why Becky felt odd or uncomfortable in her own town. There is much more

going on, and another alternative helps in explaining the incident.

(3) When one has formed friendships and they are disrupted by distance, some feelings of despondency are indeed normal. No doubt Becky was experiencing this to some degree. Although these feelings may make Becky wish she was back in the Philippines it does not explain her attitude toward her present surroundings. There is more to her feelings than this.

(4) Yes, undeniably Becky has changed. A sojourn for such a period of time as three years will have made some sort of impact as Becky had worked through many adjustments and learning processes. Doubtless some of these changes would conflict with her original environment. However, it is very unlikely that Becky would have changed so much as to never readjust to the United States.

Discussion Questions

1) How would you rate your ability to deal effectively with people from another cultural group based on your answers to the cultural incidents? Explain.

2) What does this activity indicate about facilitating favorable intercultural relations? What does this activity indicate about possible misunderstandings among people of difference cultures?

References

Brislin, R., Cushner, K., Cherrie, C., and Yong, M. 1986. *Intercultural interactions: A practical guide.* Beverly Hills, CA: Sage.

Source: Activity by Brislin, R., Cushner, K., Cherrie, C., and Yong, M. 1986. *Intercultural interactions: A practical guide.* Beverly Hills, CA: Sage.
R. Brislin, K. Cushner, C. Cherrie, and M. Yong. *Intercultural Interactions.* 2nd edition. Copyright © 1986 by Sage. Reprinted by Permission of Sage Publications, Inc.

Concept and Goal

This activity demonstrates how institutional practices, as well as individuals' attitudes, perpetuate social inequality. This activity encourages you understand how institutional forces contribute to social oppression. This is a small-group activity. In your group, respond to the eleven scenarios. Each small-group should then present the responses and prepare the discussion questions for class interaction.

Instructions

Your instructor will assign you to a group of five to six students. Your group should answer the five questions (A through E) for each of the eleven scenarios presented.

Questions

A.   Is institutional discrimination present?
B.   Against what group or groups does the practice discriminate?
C.   What is the intended purpose of each practice?
D.   Do you agree with the purpose of this practice?
E.   If the intended purpose is a valid one, how else might this purpose be achieved?

Scenarios

1.   A Hispanic actor is not given an acting role because he has a Spanish accent, and the script is written for a native english speaker.
2.   In order to be admitted into a graduate program at a college, students must score in the 80th percentile on the Graduate Record Examination (GRE).
3.   In order to become a model for a modeling agency, applicants must be 125 pounds or less.
4.   In order to qualify for a loan to buy a car, a person must have a specific minimum income and no history of paying bills late during the past ten years.
5.   An automotive company requires that its line assembly workers retire at age 65.
6.   A geography teacher shows a lot of films to her class; the class includes a blind student.
7.   A person who is confined to a wheelchair is leased an apartment, but rent rates are higher for rooms on the first floor.
8.   An adoption agency refuses to place a foster child with a family who is of a different race than the child.
9.   An elderly person must relinquish all assets in order to be admitted to a nursing home.
10.   A grocery story offers special sales on food items to large families.
11.   Couples who are mentally retarded are allowed to wed only with parental consent.

Discussion Questions

1) How do institutional practices reflect and reinforce prejudicial attitudes?

2) Does institutional discrimination always involve prejudicial intent? Explain your answer.

3) Can you think of examples of institutional racism not mentioned above? If yes, please list them.

References

Goldstein, S. B. August 1994. *Teaching the psychology of prejudice and privilege: Opportunities for active learning*. Paper presented at the 102nd Convention of the American Psychological Association. Los Angeles, CA.